THE ROAD TO KASHMIR

THE ROAD TO KASHMIR

JAMES MILNE

GYAN

Published by

Gyan Publishing House
5, Ansari Road
Daryaganj, New Delhi-110002
Phone: 011-47034999, 9811692060
E-mail: books@gyanbooks.com

Distribution Network
gyanbooks.com
India, USA, Canada, UK, Australia

ISBN: 978-93-7447-556-0 (PB)

First Published, 1925

2nd Impression 2026

Printed at: Gyan Press, Delhi.

THE ROAD TO KASHMIR
Author: JAMES MILNE

"SUMMER IN A VALE OF FLOWERS"

A Kashmir scene, near Srinagar, which well suggests the soft, caressing beauty of the Happy Valley, lying against the gaunt Himalayas.

THE ROAD TO KASHMIR

By JAMES MILNE

With a Gallery of Special Pictures

HODDER AND STOUGHTON
LIMITED LONDON

To the gracious and hospitable Moons of Kashmir—Salaam!

Who has not heard of the Vale of Cashmere
With its roses, the brightest that earth ever gave,
Its temples and grottos and fountains as clear
As the love-lighted eyes that hang over their wave?

"Lalla Rookh," by Thomas Moore.

CHAPTERS AND CONTENTS

CATALOGUE OF THE PICTURES

THE GONDOLA OF THE EAST

The Kashmiri shikara of the Jhelum River and the Dal Lake, where it can be as romantic to-day as a tale of Old Cashmere.

I. THE GREAT DIVIDE

I'll sing thee songs of Araby
And tales of fair Kashmir.

THEY are as distant from each other, the Songs of Araby and the Tales of Kashmir, as the old English ballad which they perfumed, is distant from this day and this generation. But they came together in my Eastern pilgrimage, as all things in life do come together, if you only travel far enough and long enough. True, you must watch and pray as you journey, but that is only a preparation for death, the greatest romance of life, because it is an insoluble mystery.

My ship was nosing her way through the half-grey, half-green waters of the Suez Canal. It was Sunday, and, touched by a request which a reverent Cowley Father had made to the church-goers an hour earlier, I was looking north, towards Araby. It was not at the place where you may read, in sprawling, white letters, on a big board, " Railway To Palestine," though that modern splash on the face of the desert might well make you stare, and think. It was somewhere else, it matters not where in the geography of the Suez

Canal, that I saw the vision the Cowley Father had dreamt.

What was it ? He asked us to imagine an event which might well come into the picture, where we were, between Arabia and Africa. A donkey, a dim thing in the clear sun, was on the horizon coming down the Arabian desert. Beside it walked a man, and on its back sat a woman who was hardly more than a girl. She had something on her lap, her hands holding it tenderly, and this was a child.

Joseph was the man walking alongside the donkey, Mary was the woman on its back, and it was the Infant Christ who rested in her arms. And they had so travelled nigh twenty centuries ago, away from the cruelties of Herod in Palestine, down into Egypt. Christ came this way, we were crossing His path, He had seen with His baby eyes, when they were not closed in slumber, the desert very much as we saw it, except that there was no dividing ditch called the Suez Canal.

It was a dream, become almost an actuality to the eye, there, between the sands of Araby and the sands of Egypt, for, with their dun sobriety lit by the sun, they can be eloquent. Yon speck, clear enough through one's glass, might be the Holy Pilgrimage, and indeed it had an ambling donkey, with a figure in flowing robes beside it, and a rider on its back. Suppose it to be Joseph and Mary escorting the little Christ, and you were in the hearing of the supreme, undying Song of Araby to mankind, the song of Christianity. That fancy suddenly shone to me like a flashlight upon the world of the East and the world of the West.

They say that a man or woman of the Occident who goes to the Orient never comes back the same, that some subtle change occurs in their being, making them different for ever. Something of the soul, the mind, or the body departs, as if an old friend were taken by death. Something spiritual, mental, physical, or of all the trinity arrives, a new, strange acquaintance on trial. There is a going and a coming, or one and not the other, with the same result; anyhow, a vital change has been wrought in personality.

Perhaps this is true, at least there may be some truth in it, for nothing is ever all truth, or all false, but a mixture of both. The thing is to find the key to a secret influence which, clearly, has great consequences both for individuals and for nations. It is that west of the Suez Canal Christianity inspires and directs mankind, and that east of the Suez Canal other and different religions, other and different moral codes, are in possession. That leads to the difference between the teaching of the Christ, who came down from Palestine to Egypt, and the teaching of Mohammed, Buddha, and the other founders of great religions.

Christ was the first to proclaim the sacredness of the person, the sanctity of human life, the beauty of brotherliness, everything tending to lift mankind, in this world, towards the divinity of another world. He said in so many words and every action, " I am *your* Saviour; *your* life is precious to Me; *your* life is a divine thing on earth, and so is to be guarded, revered, held sacred." Eastern religions, even the gentle Buddhism, are more communal than personal, more faiths of well-being and health, not tender about human life, callous about death. They are full of forms and incantations, exaltations and tribulations, but they go forward with the mob, with the band and the big drum, and he who falls by the way is left there.

May there not be here a key to the difference between East and West, and so a key, likewise, to what psychological change the Occidental undergoes by a visit to the Orient, much more by a stay there? Westward we practise Christ's human gospel towards each other, so far as we are able, with the consequence that our world is softer, kindlier, gentler, more understanding, more sympathetic, more brotherly than the Eastern world. No Man of the Cross hangs ever before its eyes, and so it is hard, indifferent, without individual conscience either in a spiritual or a mental sense.

Sentiment is apt to get short shrift in the Orient, as if it were an encumbrance to millions of people, so crowded together that they need every inch of space. Mortality is an easier doctrine to hold and practise, than immortality, and the climate favours it by quick burials. Reality walks the highways and poetry shrinks into the byways, as one escapes a too torrid Indian sun. A natural law is accepted without objection, or qualification, or any softening, in fullness of contract with the human being. If whatever gods there be decree it, why should anybody do other than accept it, or even bow and die under it? Reality! It is the first word and the last; the welcome for life, the discharge for death. There is no apartness in the East between conduct and action, and as the one follows the other, and the two are one, indivisible, why bother about a bridge of feeling between them? It is not there.

There are no "Whys" in the East; only the poor faith "What will be will be, and devil take the hindmost." No middle course holds with the Gods of the East, and there are few "Becauses," and they would not be heard in the surge of the multitude, gasping for spiritual air and choking without it. The East has colour but not romance, picturesqueness rather than beauty, opulence to the eye, starvation for body and soul. There Mother Nature is the primitive savage, red of tooth and long of claw, demanding an eye for an eye and taking it as a matter of course.

Wherefore it follows that a Western man going

East passes into a new atmosphere, alien to that of the Sermon on the Mount, in which he has hitherto dwelt. He is among strange deities as well as strange peoples, and, all unknown to himself, he changes, in thought, word, and even in deed. Eventually, nature in him adapting herself to environment, he may develop what is called a "yellow streak," and that is an outward, visible sign of change. There are a thousand ways in which he may change, all, initially, because that remote pilgrimage of the Infant Christ, with Joseph and Mary, is a great divide between the West and the East, between the Songs of Araby and the Tales of Kashmir.

II. EASTWARD HO!

They are not long, the weeping and the laughter,
Love and desire and hate;
I think they have no portion in us after
We pass the gate.

They are not long, the days of wine and roses:
Out of a misty dream
Our path emerges for a while, then closes
Within a dream.

WE only come this way once, and death is a mystery, and such is the moral, whether he meant it or not, of Ernest Dowson's verses. Their further moral, if they have one at all, is that we should make the best of life, take it richly, remembering always the old, sage advice, "Do not turn away beautiful things when they come, but accept them austerely."

Travel is a beautiful thing, and to go Eastward is a revealing thing, full of lights such as never might be on land or sea, if we did not personally discover them. They begin, in a manner, when a modern "tall ship" of John Masefield's visioning phrase—that is to say a great P. & O. liner—fresh and taut from London River, leaves Marseilles and heads south-east, through the dancing waters of the Mediterranean. For Marseilles is the active beginning of The Road to Kashmir, being Europe's jumping-off sea-port for Asia.

One sees in this French town, which Dumas and Conrad have both brought into stories, Asia and Africa and Europe all gathered on the quays, or in the famous Cannebière, where you can eat *bouillabaisse*, until you are heavy with satisfaction; and how they do eat, those Gascons! Marseilles is as busy humanly as a warm southern sun will let it be, and short, stocky, dark-moustached men with quick eyes and good-humoured faces toil, so that brunette women, with full figures and dainty feet may be *soignée* and smiling. It gives you the feeling of a city which would often like to make holiday, but has to make a living. It has learned to labour, if not always to wait patiently, and no liner bound East does that, but sails at the appointed hour, with a world of people in its many mansions.

You cut through between the French Corsica of Napoleonic associations, and the Italian Sardinia, which knew Garibaldi, and you come to Stromboli, on its island, with a cap of white cloud winding round its head like a handkerchief. Stromboli is active all the time, and therefore has the thunderbolt which loads every volcano, sullen or violent. But, apparently, it is unhurting, for a little town, clean and silvery to the eye, clings to

AN ALTAR
OF INDIA

The Buddha Temple, old as B.C., at Budh Gaya, intimately associated with the Prophet's "Great Renunciation" and "Enlightenment."

one of its sides and carries on, undisturbed. It has the spirit of good wine to give it confidence, because some of the choicest Italian vintages come from grapes grown on the volcanic slopes of Stromboli.

Probably you pass the more tragic Etna in the evening, when the lights are up in Messina and there is a long shimmer, like diamonds become fairies, on the Sicilian shore. To enter the Straits of Messina is to encounter the fearful Scylla and Charybdis of the ancient mariners, who steered, naked-eyed, by the planets and remained brave men. Our ship took no account of the swirling waters, though, indeed, they had an oily and dangerous face, with a suggestion of most mighty power. With long heaves they attacked her man-made steel bulwarks and then fell away with an angry hiss, and the beat of the oil-driven engines never varied.

You can persuade yourself—and it is good to do so, if you have sleepless watches of the night—that the chorus of the liner's engines and her screw are music worth the hearing. At first it is a hoarse generality, but gradually, by listening, you can find it a solo, a duet, an opera, or even a symphony. Why not?

You are in intimate communion with one of the supreme manifestations of the Supreme Will, the sea, which is life or death, or both, and everything between the two. So the elements of music are necessarily present, and Wagner might have dreamt his most tempestuous pieces in the troubled, surging, moaning Straits of Messina. Etna, rising overhead, rarely quite uncovers herself from a pall of smoke and cloud. When she does, she makes a picture of singular majesty and beauty, far removed from her mood when she overwhelmed Messina in 1908, and strewed the fair land and the poetic sea with death.

The sun grows redder and warmer as we slip towards the Orient, of which Port Said is a herald. It is a port for Egypt and a harbour of exchange between West and East, and you hear, in somebody's whisper, that it is a far better place than it once was. The travellers of two worlds meet and salaam each other here, and then go on their several ways and pilgrimages. It has a famous store where you may buy, without haggling, as with private vendors, almost anything, from the proverbial needle to the proverbial anchor. Everybody, whether come from the West or the East, has forgotten something, or wants something, and hies to the universal bazaar of Port Said, which has not many other attractions.

Grey and drab are the houses, and on every side the casualness of the East begins to show itself. But the natives, Egyptians chiefly, of many kinds, have picturesqueness in their tawny faces, in their cloaks of various colours, and in their gestures, especially the turbaned little children.

Notice that big, black soldier leading a small girl with one hand and a small boy with the other. He is taking them to school, and fierce and war-like as he looks, they are in very tender company. Even a milk-laden donkey lazily turns its head to salute them, and a man selling ducks smiles upon them with all his ebony face and a splendid set of teeth.

The Suez Canal! You hear sailor men who have gone through it and back again many times, call it "The Ditch." But its water is not ditchy in colour, and you can even fancy it a mixture of two blues, that of the Mediterranean and that of the Red Sea. It washes against an illimitable, low, flat land, called The Desert, which varies from brown sand to scrub-covered soil, wherein are some small qualities of nutriment. We discover a new version of the old passage about the Desert and the Sown, for the Suez Canal is the sower, in that it is the carrier, of many things.

Steamers before, steamers behind, steamers tied up so that an urgent one carrying the mails, may get through. And, apparently, those which tie up are those going against the tide, for, otherwise, they would not have straight holding and, swinging, might impede the narrow way. Brown men in waist-cloths on the steamers, lots of them, with bodies ripened into rich shades of tan by the plenteous Asiatic sun. Ashore, camels burdened with goods and, now and then, a motor-car flying along the road beside the canal. Arabs labouring and Arabs idling and talking, for the water-way which De Lesseps dreamt and drove has always to be defended against the sands of the desert, and, moreover, it is constantly being widened.

A witty American has remarked of the Statue of Liberty, in New York Bay, that it turns its back on America. Most statues either suggest something stupid or are themselves uninspired, and certainly that of De Lesseps, at the European entrance to his Suez Canal, is a poor affair. Its stature does not at all suggest the stature for which he and his work stand in the world. It is really he who brings together, for our view, that Arab bidding his camel get down on its belly among the sands, so that its bales of wool shall be unloaded; and here, in "The Ditch," a liner which is a floating town in population and a first-class hotel in luxury.

Surely the man who married those unlike services of the ancient and the modern world, was a genius in imagination and in achievement. Which, when you think it over, suggests that he did not need any monument, because he is bigger than any monument could be, unless, perhaps, the Pyramids over there in Egypt, to which country you will soon be saying Good-bye.

III. THE SONG OF THE RED SEA

I'll borrow life and not grow old
And nightingales and trees
Shall keep me, though the veins be cold,
As young as Sophocles:
"Ionica," by William Cory.

IT is the spirit that matters when you travel, especially when you take the Eastward Road to old, eternal things which are new to you. A spirit with the curiosity of youth, a mind with youth's elasticity, a body which finds a stimulus, like youth come again, in new skies and earths and seas. Those are the right equipments, and, when they are there, wise Mother Nature soon harmonises them to their fresh settings, even to the fabled Red Sea.

Why is it called that? Its atmosphere sometimes has that touch, but its waters are dark blue, with ribbons of white splashing in the breeze, when there is one! While we are passing through the Bitter Lakes, an old traveller in those parts says, "I can remember when we got ashore here and bathed. Similarly we got ashore in the Canal, when our steamers were tied up, and vastly amused ourselves by riding donkeys. Old times, old ways; all gone, alas!" And he meant it, for human nature is such that we like most the things of our youth, especially when we grow old and they are dead.

"No more donkeys," he went on, "or perhaps there simply isn't time for them, but the Bitter Lakes have lost none of their salt flavour, and I'll bet if you were to jump overboard you could not sink. Only there are two dangers, because every unusual act has its dangers. Your feet would be thrown higher by the water than your head, an awkward position, certainly when there are sharks about. So if you must, in a frolicsome spirit, leap overboard, don't stay more than a moment or two. If you do you may leave a big toe, shall we say, in a mouth of fearsomely sharp teeth."

All this was said blithely, as old-timers recall the past, but clearly the passage of the Red Sea, apart from the Scriptural one, must once have been fuller of adventures and peradventures, of reality and romance, than it is to-day, when you cannot see Mount Ararat because it is not in sight. It lies somewhere away to the north, and even if it did not lie anywhere on earth, its name would still be a symbol for rest after storm, for deliverance after peril, and so a slogan to mankind in his pilgrimage.

A "hot weather" day in the Red Sea! It comes in freshly, with a good spank of wind and a cheery tumble of white wherever the eye wanders. Beyond rises the head of a brass nail, and this is the Eastern sun opening his eyes for the day. He, like all creation, needs a little time to make his toilet, and if he were a woman, not a man, he would naturally need longer. As it is, he winks his bleary eyes at the Red Sea saying its Matins, then looks steadily and afar on it, and soon brings its surface back to the hot glister at which he left it the night before.

Gradually the clouds of the morning evaporate into little wisps, like puffs of tobacco smoke from an Indian hookah. They may scatter into a thin veil, lining the sky, or they may disappear, tired of the growing heat. By now that heat is in possession of the whole sky, the Red Sea, and the ship, or so you feel. If there be a following wind, instead of a head wind, the poor voyager is grilled like a cutlet and served up like a curry, Bengal, Malay, or what sort you will.

Hotly, drowsily, the afternoon draws towards evening, without incident to the indifferent eye, unless it be the passing of another ship, miles away, across those endless waters, always moving on top, still as dead life many fathoms down. Or there may be a cry, " Here go porpoises," and you watch them, browny-green, wobbly things, against the azure waves, swimming and diving in the wake of the ship. You might think them children let out to amuse themselves, and in that way to amuse you. Actually they are hungering for the many crumbs which go overboard from a vessel, because, like Mother Nature's whole brood, they are ever hungry. But suddenly they are gone, and a sailor knows why, for, with his sharp eye, he has caught, in their midst, the grey flick of a shark's fin, a razor-blade piercing the water.

The shark is also piloting for food, and it may be seen, again and again, claiming a right of way which other fishes readily grant. Comes the swift darkness, and it is lost, as the ocean itself is lost against the disappearing sun. He has had his day, hot and blazing, but he seems loath to give up his Oriental kingdom of waters and earth, even for a few hours, and hangs on, scoring the horizon with lamps of many colours.

Blue is for " I go," and it has the soft tear which ever moistens a farewell. Purple is for " I am going," and it radiates into a bonfire which embellishes, for a moment, the world being left, and must, surely, light the world being possessed. Saffron, with a dark veil blotting it out, is for " Good-night," and the sea and the wind answer " Good-night," " Good-night ! "

Then the stars come out from their high vault, and how cool and wonderful they seem, where the sun boiled all the day, and what an array of them ! They nod and blink and dazzle, they bow and salute and dance, they make strings of diamonds and pearls on the neck and bosom of loving Mother Night. Kings and queens of the West,

LOOKING WESTWARD !

An Indian lady of quality in a charming blend of the sari and the modern vogue of Europe.

sultans and sultanas of the East, may have gorgeous jewels and wear them gorgeously. But no mortal was ever arrayed like this Mother Night, star-scattered in the heavens above the Red Sea.

Her treasury there is beyond price and beyond avarice, because it is a divine diadem with which God has crowned the earth. It is a greater glory which is not material, and so it cannot be had and held as if it were a body. It is a spirit, a soul, a mind, a heart, and only by simplicity, by faith, by beauty, may you understand it; for the stars hate the garish day of envy, malice, and unworthiness.

That is why they choose the night, which is cool and sweet and healing, as if an Indian ayah were hushing a child which has stormed all day, into a long, gentle sleep. Children are born free-men, rebels against being cribbed on land or cabined afloat, but they tire, as their elders do. Then the star-lit night of Eastering waters takes them softly into dreamland, until the morning.

IV. THE WAY OF A SHIP

By faith they passed through the Red Sea, as by dry land: which, the Egyptians assaying to do, were drowned.—Hebrews xi. 29.

But as for you, turn you and take your journey into the wilderness by the way of the Red Sea.—Deuteronomy i. 40.

WE are all Israelites when we travel, because travel worthy of the name carries a certain risk, and Jehovah is not always about, to withstand the Egyptians. Perhaps one can take a journey into the wilderness, which is to say the unknown, by the way of the Red Sea as fully as that can be done anywhere else. Humanly, surely, for amusing people are to be met on a great liner, thrashing through an indulgent sea, a burnished sun, and a languishing moon.

Our company of men and women, brought together by the chance that they were all going East, began with the commander, grave but bending, and ended with the Lascars, picturesque in white cotton trousers, bluish jackets, and caps of as many colours as Joseph's Scriptural coat. Between the bridge and their quarters, lodged somewhere and somehow, there was a whole community of people. Shall we sample it?

An American girl going out to an American husband, who was, it appeared, in business in Calcutta. She was a girl in years, but a wife, as she told us, almost at the first meal, perhaps to let us know there was a statute of limitations. She did not want to be out of any fun going; a forenoon lounge in a sun-warmed chair, with company; the "ship sweep," and its excitement at noon; the afternoon cup of tea with its light gossip and earnest curiosity about everybody; the joyful after-dinner dance; or even a stroll on deck in the Asiatic night. But there was John waiting on the Bund at Bombay, American John, not much of a lover, perhaps, because, one gathered, he was unsophisticated, yet a "regular fellow," and to be treated regularly.

Therefore all the smart Paris dresses her young ladyship of America trotted out, were merely given an airing for ultimate John. All the, no doubt, equally smart et ceteras in the way of toilet, about which she gave us hints, were also the inheritance of John, lucky young man. Miss Columbia—for we refused to say "Mrs."—was so easy, so frank, so natural, so good, yet so lovably naughty, that she was soon in high favour with everybody.

She, like the rest of us, speculated much over the young man who had a stunning wife, fair, elegant, glinting of eye and pearly of teeth, and who yet, himself, could do no better with his face than wear two patches of woolly beard on it. Curly hair, clear, clean eyes, an excellent nose, a face of quality and intelligence, winding up with a chin clad in faint straggling patches of mouse-coloured wool. It was almost Montmarterish, but his native English tongue put that out of the question.

He danced beautifully, better even than his young wife, but her line and grace of limb made up for that. We never solved the mystery of the woolly chops on a face which would have been better without them, unless the chin was weak and had to be hidden. But we were unanimous that the wife should have turned Delilah, in a beardish way, and shorn them in her husband's sleep.

Again there was the tall lady, thin and elegant, and the tall husband, stout and roast-beefish, compared with her fineness. A newly married couple, we heard, and to see her stroke his cheek, while they leant across a bridge-table during a minute's absence of the other partners, was to still believe in honeymoons. She had wonderful eyes, and could use them in order not only to see, but to be seen. They looked out beneath a broad, rather low brow, down which there ran the frontage of a half-curly, half-smooth head of hair. The dark eye-brows were arched, with an arch which might have been made in Japan, and the lady and her husband were outward bound for that land. But the high cheek-bones suggested, maybe, a touch of Muscovy, just as the lips, plain in the day, red-rouged at night, suggested Paris.

Certainly my lady's frocks were Parisian in their mixture of languor and smartness, their high-lights and low-lights of colour, their caress of a beautiful body and the evident stimulation they were to a sensitive spirituality and a broad mentality. Ah! here was a woman meant to walk a quarter-deck with the winds about her, or dally silkily in a boudoir, doing the little things which do not matter, or matter greatly. Women in their bedrooms and their boudoirs, alone, unseen, secluded from their men-folk, are the mothers of the children who play in nurseries, because they, also, will be marshalling and re-marshalling the pretty things of life.

You may always wonder, and there is no place where it is more in order than on board a ship full of passengers. There was, again, the elegant lady who bossed and managed her husband so deftly that he did not know it. Was she French? She had the French woman's flair for colour in dress, something daring yet austere, something that never failed to suit her ivory-like personality. It seemed curiously in contrast with the heavy, "cave" sort of man whom she wound round her fingers, but, no doubt, beauty and the strong animal do have affinities, especially when beauty goes bare-legged on the ship's deck. Hot? Of course; but it was a very white-skinned leg.

Other people: the confirmed bachelor who wanted to reduce marriage to the level of a game of bridge; the Anglo-Irishman who had an hour in one camp and an hour in the other; the Scotsman who made his own Scots stories and found them all humorous; the men who were good fellows, though most at home in the smoking-room; the women who had babies and smiled constantly; and the women who had none and so were in danger of being waspish in tongue, snobbish in behaviour, and lanternish of jaw.

Life sails the sea, as well as walks the earth, and it is ever worth while to encounter colour of character, variety of temperament, and generosity of movement. Ever, too, there is a chance of a private drama, and that, in the enveloping blaze of the Red Sea, can be diverting.

Thus the grave, elderly General at the other end of the table had, clearly, been rather disapproving of the Calcutta-bound, lively American lady at our end. Possibly he was not sure if she was as good as she should be, for there was the damning evidence of her gaiety and her wit and those Paris frocks. There is, you know, the kind of wise man, who thinks like this, until he finds he is on the wrong track, and then he is sorry, awkward, apologetic.

One evening the General, really a most chivalrous Sahib, was down early to dinner, and the American lady happened along a minute afterwards. Now was his opportunity to atone, to be nice, to greet her with, " A pleasant evening, is it not ? " She, remembering his previous silences and resenting them, would not hear him. " We are getting on very well," he tried again, referring to the voyage, but she was not listening. A third effort, with, by this time, the table stewards keen on the heels of the drama, and then he gave up the battle.

" He deserved it," said she, but we knew that his slow English way of understanding women, and his clumsy atonement, had been his undoing. She probably also knew that, for she had not been without " experience of men," as she put it herself once, when John, waiting at Bombay, was mentioned. It worried her that he had not wirelessed her on the ship, because she felt that omission a want of homage. Now, there was a Jamie who had always understood her, American though he was, and who never, never failed with a telegram or a bunch of flowers, or anything else.

When the sun went down on the Red Sea she prayed for Jamie, in far America, she prayed for her mother, there also, and she counted the suns that would bring her to John, because; well, because they hadn't been married long, hadn't seen much of each other, and she had a woman's wonder as well as a woman's experience.

V. AN OUTPOST OF THE RAJ

Let the household hold together,
though the house be ne'er so small;
Strip the rice-husk from the rice-grain
and it groweth not at all:

Indian Poem.

IT was queer to be reading this at the moment we came to Aden, for here the Eastern wisdom found a practical illustration in a Western way. Aden is small, but, in ill weather and good, it has toughly held to the world household which we call the British Empire. A spacious business, when you think it out, leaning over the bulwarks of the ship and saying again to yourself, "So this is Aden. Well!"

It strikes your eye as a craterous place, and that is just what it is, for two old craters form a series of rocky peninsulas. Never a tree, only a touch of grass where the English longing for a lawn has caused a few blades to grow near the club. But then Aden has only from three to five inches of rainfall in a year, and so it has mostly to rely upon getting its drink by condensation from the surrounding sea.

There were, of old, people in those parts who

A BURIED CÆSAR

The Tomb, splendid in red stone and white marble, of Akbar, the Great Mogul, near Agra and the familiar Taj Mahal.

also needed water and could not condense it from the sea; therefore they hewed great tanks in the rocky land and let these catch what mercies fell from the heavens. The tanks still exist, but if Aden were dependent on them it would go very dry, and its temperature, for most parts of the year, can be pretty infernal.

Sun-sun-sun! More sun-sun-sun! And yet again sun-sun-sun. What parchment for a grey morning in England, or a Scotch mist up in the northern kingdom! Even so, you are told that Aden isn't a bad place to live in, that it has a society which can be amusing, though limited, and that it had dancing most evenings. Queer that dancing should be the oldest natural pastime on the earth, or one of the oldest, and yet always the newest. But no, not queer, because it is an expression of the elements in men and women which make them seek each other.

A small colony of English-speaking people is held up, so to speak, on this Aden, a sun-burned area of seventy-five square miles. The island of Perim in the Straits of Bab-el-Mandeb is a relation, in the sense that it is part of the Aden Settlement. But it is even less hospitable, as, maybe, the Abyssinians, the Persians, and, later, the Turks found, when they were masters of Araby by the sea. You need imagination to bring them back in all their colour, but the Somalis, men and women, who make so active a picture in the life of modern Aden, suggest how rich and varied that colour must have been.

Handsome fellows the Somalis, handsome women the Somali lassies, both copper-brown, like old bronzes, or black, like night on the Indian Ocean, when the day suddenly dies in the noose of the pendant night. The men come over from their corner of the African Continent with such merchandise as they have to trade, and you watch their heavily-laden boats making for the Aden anchorage. Primitive boats, primitive sailors, but they belong to the picture, and you linger on it.

Nearer, a team of dark Somali brethren, happy, smiling, will be " oiling up " your steamer from a tank away in the distance, which pours its liquid fuel through a long pipe floated on the sea by barrels. They are Somalis, in loin cloths and not much more, who have found work in Aden, like many Somali girls turned domestic servants and nurses. The East is a place of service and servants, and when Westerners return home, they must feel as if they had lost a ministering kingdom.

The smell of coffee and gums, of spices and feathers may be forgotten as so much poetry of Araby or India. But it is another matter when the loss is the swift black feet of attendance at Aden, or the gentle brown feet of willingness in India. The aloes of Socotro may be so far away that they flavour life no more, but the dark hands that handled them are of a good-service legion regretted as well as lost.

When a Vienna lady asks for a cup of Mocha, as she does, she cannot fancy what her words would mean to one who has spent years where Mocha gives an Arabian salute to the Red Sea and to Aden. It sits there, on the road to India, which changes, however, with the coming of air-power, as a vital thing in a new world. How quickly this new world does wag! If Marco Polo were again alive and were to go East on his travels, there would be many surprises along his path—great ships, as comfortable as houses; swift trains, carrying every luxury with them; aeroplanes and motor-cars; cables and telegrams to keep him informed about mankind everywhere.

Aden is a rocky pivot on which something of all that turns, and so we threw coins to the diving Somalis, and watched the manifold ways of native life as it attended our passing craft. Turbaned heads, heads swathed in mere cloths of every hue, bare feet as shapely as you could wish to see, gartered legs, not because there were stockings to keep in place, but as a talisman to keep away the plague and other ills of the flesh. Aden is a hotch-potch of Eastern life, ancient and modern, in a pot of small size, and it boils both hotly and briskly there on its sentinel rocks 'twixt the Red Sea and the Indian Ocean.

" Popular with English soldiers," said somebody, and to the wondering question " Why ? " came the answer, " Because it is generally the last station on the road home from Eastern service." Ah, Atkins likes to get home ; home, where he is understood and understands ; home, to his mother, if he has one, for he never loses that sentiment. He will have seen a Hindu wife salute her husband in the morning by putting her hands prettily together and bowing ever so slightly. My master, my lord, my deity ! It is a remnant of the Indian wife's way to salvation, by devotion to her husband and the one-time funeral pyre.

Atkins, on sentry-go, at Aden, has no use for this sort of nonsense, but he knows his mother waits for him in England and will worship him when they meet. Just like the Indian wife and her husband ; merely different in the process and the people concerned. Atkins must not stay too long in the East—and regulations take care of that —because to overstay might mean a funeral at sea, as on the last homeward voyage of our own ship.

Somebody had been long, too long, in India, and had travelled from Calcutta to Bombay in the heat of a brutal thirty-six hours. The doctors had told him he must, for his health's sake, hasten to temperate England. He sent his wife and his family ahead, wound up his affairs, counting the daily risk and taking it, and then was ready. He came on to the ship rather exhausted, and that night, as he was getting into his bed, died from a heart seizure.

Next morning the vessel stopped dead for a minute, the commander spoke a soft word of committal, and a little bundle of canvas, loaded with lead, shot into the Indian Ocean. It has known many burials like that, the East taking its tribute of human life from the West. No storm of triumph does it raise, nor hurricane of grief, but just it rolls on, indifferent to everything except that it is the open water-road to India.

VI. LIFE ON THE INDIAN WAVE

To him who travels with a goal worth proving
What matter the conditions of his roving ?
The temple floor shall be a palace to him,
The stony heath a feather-bed to woo him,
And leathery scraps, which stay-at-homes abhor,
Shall be to him a banquet and much more.

Eastern Wisdom.

ONE wonders, among wonders both growing and fading, whether the modern comfort of travel has not taken away some of its tang. Suffering is a preface to every great joy, if only as a sting to sharpen that joy when it comes. Make travel luxury, and you throw out most of the odes to it, Eastern or Western, though you may still quote them for what they were and to make a contrast.

Now what would the Indian Ocean have been like, experienced on an old-time tea-clipper, with the sun molten, and never a breath of wind ? A floating and a tight little hell, and the high heavens mocking its swelter ! Ordinarily a ship makes its own breeze by moving through the air, but with a following wind this ceases, and there is simply a stifling envelopment. Hot air, sweat, horridness ;

you might be in a Turkish bath. And yet it was where the Red Sea ends and the Indian Ocean goes on that a whale, strayed from cooler seas, once met a red death. It is a sailor's story, a true one of the sea, and it has never been told except in shipboard conversation.

A liner, now old, but still remembered for her smartness, was making the homeward Indian voyage, and it was early morning. The captain was lying down in his berth near the bridge, and the first officer was in charge. He gave a sudden cry of surprise, the ship hit something with a heavy thud, and the captain, leaping on to the bridge, saw a strange sight. A huge whale had been cut clean through by the sharp bow of the steamer, and its halves were streaming away on each side, amid waves red with its blood.

A queer, butchery business, was it not? The fish had risen to spout as the liner came on it, and thus had not been seen sooner. You can, from the bridge of a modern tall ship, see the Indian Ocean for twenty miles around, when visibility is good. You, yourself, stand beside a most delicate web of machinery, which exercises man's control over the endless range of waters, for such it appears. Deep waters, too, with only the leap of a flying fish, or the tumble of a porpoise, to move them now, but a tumult in the season of the monsoon.

Angry currents, cross seas, heavy rollers, rain,

wind and darkened heavens! That, the sailor man tells you, is the monsoon, when the portholes are closed and everything that could be shaken loose is made fast. You marvel, feeling the sweet, soft day it is, how the monsoon can be so angry and, still more, how a master mariner's governance of it can be so complete.

Wonderful devices let him know with exactitude just what his ship is doing at every moment: the revolutions of the screw; the speed of her movement; the angle of the voyage; the state of the oil-tanks, if she is an oil-burner; the trimness of all the lights, or the failure of one; what's doing in the engine-room, between which and the bridge there is a telephone whose handle you place against your throat, not your ear; the closing of the bulkhead doors, in case of emergency; or the far flash of a searchlight on the road through the dark waters and the dark night.

Western man has found many saving and conquering devices since he first broke into those Indian waters. But they still have their mysteries and their dangers, for God is the high admiral of the seas, and He ordains and orders. Did you notice that white sail on the far horizon? It is a little Indian *dhow*, bound from India, probably Bombay, to some place on the African coast. If everything goes well, the voyage will, maybe, take two months time. If everything does not go well, no more will be heard of that *dhow* or what

A SACRED
HINDU CITY

Princely mansions of Benares, on the banks of the Holy Ganges, where its religious life finds picturesque expression.

fate overtook it. Simply, venturing Indian fellows have taken the risk of carrying a cargo over a great ocean, sunburnt or monsooned:

From Comorin to Ormuz, Mombassa to Bombay,
Ploughing through the seaways as in da Gama's day.
Loaded to the gun'l with their topsides cane and
clay.
Just the same old hookers in just the same old way.

If they get through—and mostly they do—it is a victory over Mother Sea, and if they do not get through, it is a lost battle. Water is the essential thing, because life without it to drink is impossible, and an Indian *dhow* cannot carry very much. Its crew have to be rationed from the first, and steamers know that to happen within signalling distance of this kind of craft is to be asked first for water, and then for anything else.

Dhows are the mendicants of the Indian Ocean, and it is possible that the watch of a steamer does not always see them, just as Nelson had a blind eye for a famous signal. Distress, life in peril? Then it is S.O.S., but to stop on a small account is to lose time, and that is another matter. A mental hail and farewell is all that is possible, with the sailor's prayer for other sailors, "God be your compass."

With visibility and a good ship the Indian Ocean is tractable, and it has lots of sea-room. But it may surprise you to be told that a sailoring anxiety of the long voyage from London to India is its coast-wising. Only for a few days, which are not all consecutive, is a ship absolutely free from shore entanglements. A captain wants the freedom of the seas in a typhoon, and a lee shore, however distant, is no desired thing then. However, every ocean has its own joys and its own evils, whether you choose the spice-scented waters of Asia, or the bracing waters, subject to fogs and ice, which link North America with Europe. Similarly, every one has its own expressions: the bubbling phosphorescence of the Mediterranean, the blue, aerated sparkle of the Atlantic, or the white, curly laceyness of the Indian Ocean.

Sail north, " to Norroway o'er the faem," and a summer day lingers long with you, giving you a witching twilight. Sail east, and the sun goes down with a run; so quickly, in fact, that darkness comes before you have realised it. The sun setting on the Indian Ocean is, every night, a picture in colours and a drama in surprises. You may see it as a silver temple, against a sky flecked with cloudy handkerchiefs; as a golden ball, ruddy, like war rolling along a field of red; or as a clearly outlined ship's-hull, with masts and sails, burning fiercely to the water line and then sinking into blackness.

" Oh, how wonderful!" came a musical voice across the deck the night that sun-ship sank, and it was the voice of a young Indian lady whom we had been admiring in the heat of the day. Every body had now, in token of it, shed the last garment, short of decency, which, in the East, is also reached by the way of nakedness, for there is purity where there is no mystery. The European women looked raw-edged, out of their element, but the Indian women, in their bright, light clothes, were animated, very all alive.

Our particular Indian lady wore a *sari* of cool, green silk, and it made her look cool. She had green slippers, trimmed with gold, and her feet were bare. Such dainty feet, they looked, as, unconsciously, she poked them out and into the slippers. They had not a corn or a wart or anything else upon them but were soft and dimpled, like a child's feet, and oh, so expressive! Truly, she was an Eastern Lucy Grey, for—

Her feet beneath her petticoat,
Like little mice stole in and out.

VII. THE GATEWAY TO INDIA

Neither by service nor fee
Came I to mine estate—
Mother of Cities to me,
For I was born in her gate,
Between the palms and the sea,
Where the world-end steamers wait.

Kipling's " Dedication to the City of Bombay."

ONE might say of Bombay that it has the picturesqueness of the East with the kindliness of the West, and that therefore it is, on mere sight, a likable city. It is, among other things, Rudyard Kipling's city, for he was born there, and so it has made its own great contribution to the English literature of our day and generation.

Bombay built a temple called the Gateway of India, which opened first for King George and Queen Mary when they went to the Delhi Durbar, and which opens again for a coming or a departing Viceroy. This Gateway is the sea door, the front door of Bombay, as well as of India, and you should behold the human colour around it on one of the many holidays which invite the Parsees, the Hindus, or the Mohammedans, to wear their dandiest clothes.

What a crowd of men and women and small children !—hundreds and thousands of them, and all on the move: sober-looking men, old or middle-aged; dignified wives and mothers to correspond; young men, some of them as gay as you like—" knuts " we should have called them once; and young women with smiles behind the timidity of sex. That is holiday Bombay natively, and you see working Bombay natively, the moment you descend from your ship on to the noisy, busy Apollo Bundar.

It is a hive of workers, for the coming of the weekly mail-boat is a high event, not only for Bombay, but for the whole of India. Its passengers will quickly be distributed all over the country by special trains, and its tons of home letters will go with them, or on their heels. You are to remain a little in Bombay, fortunately, if you have never visited it before, unfortunately if you are for another part of India and have to await a ship or a train to take you there.

Probably the heat, if the time be any time except from November to March, is pretty bad, and pretty humid, a weary kind of heat to abide. The only thing to do is to wear as light clothes as possible, and those of the right kind of material. You may have been well enough advised to bring them with you, but you may not, in which case you must expect to pay a good price for them in Bombay, because your English taste is sure to demand English quality, and that means an import duty on top of the home price.

Myself, I walked ashore in Bombay with a proper "Bombay bowler," otherwise a khaki-coloured pith topi, and this, awaiting friends assured me, was an almost unheard-of thing. A charming aide-de-camp said it was such a relief not to have to race off to the nearest shop for the absolutely necessary topi. But you will go wrong if you take only white drill suits to India, because Europeans there, nowadays, mostly wear coloured clothes of the tussore kind. They are better to the eye than mere white, they are lighter in texture and more porous, and of course they do not so earnestly invite dirt.

If you are bidden to the famous Bombay Yacht Club you can put aside your "bowler," for that is a place of coolness as well as of company, of shade as well as of good-fellowship. But you need it whenever you come into the hard blister of the Indian sun, and you marvel how graceful native women, with only filmy scarves to protect their heads, can withstand its fierceness.

Notice that woman of the people with a bundle on her head, features of dark bronze, like ebony, a bust like a Venus, hips that move to a song and a simple wrap around them. It falls modestly to where her knees pass to shapely legs, elegant ankles, and small feet. She might be a statue come to life and movement, but she is unconscious of her Indian woman's beauty, and only bent on her domestic business, whatever it may be.

Bombay is full of Indian human types, and, for that reason, among others, a doubly accredited Gateway to India. Sit you down, if you can find a seat somewhere, and watch the throng of humanity. White for the body, colour for the head, are the wear of the Indian man, who is less interested in you than you are in him. But, then, you are new to "India's coral strand," and he, perhaps, has seen many a European come and go. When you have satisfied your human curiosity, go your way to the friends, known or only now to be known, who will make you welcome.

The true Briton who has made Bombay his home for long, welcomes you as a brother, nay, with the warmth of a long-lost brother. A gifted and beautiful Parsee lady, the learned correspondent of a dear, scholarly friend of yours in England, takes you into the bosom of her family and gives you tea and much good talk. Her mother shares in it, and so does an aunt whose face is softly sympathetic and who wears the Parsee *sari* with particular grace.

Most distinguished of all is the head of the household, a veteran man of affairs and knowledge, whom the King-Emperor has delighted to knight. His library of the East, filled with English books, covering the world of wisdom, might be the library of the other veteran friend in the West, whose ambassador you have been. Strange, isn't it, that East and West should seem so very alike in individuals? And yet it is not strange, for all the life-roads of study and simplicity lead upward and onward.

Thus goes the day, or several days in Bombay: kindness and colour everywhere, from a shopping street in the heart of the town to Malabar Hill, its wealthy and fashionable quarters; from a modest flat, in a tree-shaded street, to Government House, on a point of land which the sea guards from invasion. It has been a seat of government for many of the years we have shaped the destinies of India, maybe with varying wisdom, but always with sincerity and always with tolerance for the religions and customs of its different and sharply divided peoples.

The Towers of Silence, where the Parsees lay out their dead and the waiting vultures consume them, are their own testimony to this wisdom of the Raj in India. The Ghats, where the Hindus burn their dead on wooden pyres, are another evidence of the same broad-minded rule; the acceptance even of the forms of eternity. Here are places which give Bombay a peculiar name and fame, so shall we visit them, and do it with the reverent mind they should command, because the

AN INDIAN
RELIGIOUS FESTIVAL

At a certain season of the year, thousands of Hindus make pilgrimage to the various sacred rivers and the temples beside them.

parting between the quick and the dead, whatever be the ceremony, is an event sacred to all mankind and to all the gods that be.

Zoroaster is the God who inspires the Towers of Silence, and his teaching dominates the ritual which the Parsees practise there. You arrive, after a swift though rather a long drive, at gates which open into what might be a well-wooded, well-flowered, well-kept garden, set on a spacious incline. You are met by Parsee guides, who take you round this religious reservation, pointing out the several Towers of Silence and explaining the burial uses of each. One is reserved for certain old Parsee families, another is for the dead who have come by accident or violence, the rest are for those, generally, who belong to the Parsee faith.

You are not allowed into the Towers, which is understandable, but your view of them from some way distant is completed by an explanatory model which shows their interior construction. Similarly, it illustrates the manner of laying out the bodies on a sort of grille and the resting there of the bones, left by the vultures, until the sun has crumbled them into dust, which water carries back to earth that bore it. A Hill of Calvary, you may call this churchyard of the Parsees, who are mostly located in Bombay, where they are a very wealthy, very influential section of the community. But it is also a Mount of Olives, because it breathes freshness, being set high above Bombay, and because it has the tree and flower scents of a Garden of Eden.

Around the battlements of yonder Tower of Silence there is a file of large, grey birds, motionless, their beaked heads falling low between their wings, as if they were asleep. They have gorged themselves, an hour ago, on some corpse, and they are listless and heavy. Or they may just be waiting for a body, mourners who will feast, and meanwhile seem like mutes in mourning, and certainly are birds of ill-omen, because they are the scavengers of death.

One vulture moves lazily, slowly, on the tower walls, lifts himself into the air with his huge wings, and flies about in a slow circle, as if he were on patrol duty for the whole company. His movement, as one's Parsee guide points out, is exactly that of a modern aeroplane; not with jerks and jumps, like many birds, but evenly, planing upward or downward, balancing flat on the wing, or making a swift curve in this direction or that. Then, having done his patrol, he drops lazily back to his place in the dark, grey line manning the rampart of his Tower of Silence. There he slumbers, but does not sleep, except in the night, when death itself must wait on the funeral of next day.

One learns grimly that the vultures clean a body

to the bone, in two hours from the time it is put in their charge by the relatives of the man or woman, boy or girl, who was once alive. The birds never leave their hill of death, but are born, grow up, and spend their lives there, keeping the last watch, for the Parsee quick, on the Parsee dead. They have, from their Towers of Silence, the finest view of Bombay, lying spread out below. A glow of the Indian sun lingers on that view, and you carry it away with you, braided by a line of grey shadows, waiting, waiting, waiting!

Fire is the redeeming instrument of Hinduism, and hence the burning Ghats of Bombay and other parts of India. They have the atmosphere of raw finality, of something finished, and so without sentiment, or hope, which is characteristic of native India. You have lived, and you have done with your life what you could, what the chaos of the cosmos or the humours of the fates permitted you to do. It has been an affair which you did not seek, which you were not consulted about, which, perhaps, you could have well been without altogether, though that would have been not to live at all.

Now another stage, static and called death, has arrived, and it is taken with the same philosophy; even, it may be, without thought, except the Eastern "Kismet." Anyhow, as it was life, and the affairs of life, mostly petty and worrying, so it is death and the affairs of death, which are still less important, and therefore fitly pass away in smoke of a blue-grey colour.

Those are the thoughts and impressions which assail you at the Ghats of Bombay, on the morning of your visit to them. A wide, rough gateway; Indian men in Indian dress, keeping ward at it; the submission of your credentials to be there and the invitation to walk inward so far and no farther, because this is holy ground. Quite near, a small company of Hindus are drowning out the embers of a pyre which has consumed their dead, and doing it with a rubber hose-pipe. Yes, that is a shock, but remember you are in the Orient, where death is not content to lie in wait for life, but seizes it as a tiger might seize and devour a man in the jungle.

A body had been tenderly placed on the piled logs, and the nearest relative had put a devotional torch to them. Soon the spirit, once tenanting that body, had gone up into the eternal heavens, and the unneeded flesh had fallen to ashes, earth returned to earth in the Hindu way. No trappings of woe, no weeping and wailing, no emotions unstrung—just plain, brutal death.

Over there was another pyre which was still red and glowing, for it had not finished its office. Gradually this glow would grow fainter, darker, and then also go out in ashes, and a new pyre for another Hindu would be built on the same spot. Thus goes the " last post " at the Burning Ghats of Bombay, and as " ghat " only means " place," it signifies the commonness of death. Merely its cerements differ among the races of mankind, from all of whom it claims a final allegiance.

VIII. A LIGHT OF ASIA

False, fragrant fatal! Krishna's quest is o'er
By Jumna's shore!
The Indian Song of Songs.

"*The illustrious sepulchre of Arjumand Banu Begham, called Mumtaz Mahal. Died in* 1040 *A.H.*" (1630 A.D.).
On the Taj Mahal tomb of Shah Jahan's Queen.

EVER since the world began men have been a divided heritage for the woman of passion and the woman of love, for Krishna of the Jumna and Mumtaz Mahal, who lighted Shah Jahan's heart when she lived and left it dark when she died. Even the Mogul Emperors, thinking women only playthings and fishing for them, dressed as silver fishes, in the scented lakes of old Indian palaces, ascended to pure love, as the Taj Mahal testifies, as well as fell to voluptuous passion, as history tells.

Blazing heat, for the sun was like burning copper and the air like a blast furnace; clouds of mosquitoes, which brigaded on one's bed curtains at night, evil, black spots scattered on innocent white; a flat, arid, sandy, desert-like landscape, with the Jumna stealing between brown, muddy banks; and strings of native people and native animals going about their business. That, with the Taj Mahal crowning, glorifying it all, is Agra, once, no doubt, the most famous city in the Plains of India.

Here the Mogul Kings, headed by Babar in 1526, and followed by Akbar and Jehangir, set their footprints on Indian soil with a definiteness which remains to-day in The Fort and in the magnificent remains of Fatehpur Sikri, twenty miles away, as well as in the Taj Mahal itself. You are on the hearthstone, cold now, so far as those who warmed it were concerned, of a blaze of colour such as the world had hardly seen before except, perhaps, in Ancient Rome, such as it has not seen since, and such as it can never, perhaps, see again.

We have red sandstone, denoting strength, white marble, denoting beauty, and the two used in a thousand ways to perpetuate the artistry which the Moguls stood for. They had half India at their feet, they could command its precious stones for their whims and its people for their serfs. What splendour, what luxury, what refinement of indulgence went on within the walls of Akbar's palace, looking down on the indifferent Jumna, then a great waterway of trade, now, in the dry season, a ribbon stealing slowly through the

Indian landscape, with only a remnant of its old picturesque traffic.

You go out to Fatehpur Sikri, if only in sentimental tribute to the reason which set Akbar to build it. His children had all died in infancy, as children die readily in India to-day, for it is a callous mother to the abundant life which it creates. Akbar wanted a son, and he went to the village of Sikri to consult a Mohammedan saint, one Shaik Salim Chisti, who lived there. " Send your wife to stay in my house," said the saint, and this was done, trustingly. She gave Akbar a son who was to be the Emperor Jehangir, father of Shah Jahan, the inspirer, the dreamer, in part, maybe, the designer of the divine Taj Mahal.

The pilgrim to Agra ever turns to it, though there is much to hold him within the long, high walls of Akbar's citadel, with its strangely insufficient name of The Fort. One associates that name with a place having military purposes and little else. Akbar built himself a stronghold above all risks and surprises, and indeed its walls, hardly touched by time, not at all by decay, might hold up a modern army.

But, soldier and artist in one personality, he also made a pleasure house of supreme perfection and delicacy. He could not be a descendant of Chengiz Khan, the Mongol, and of Tamerlane the Terrible, without wishing to secure, in his private hours, the rewards of what he had won on

the battlefield. Nor could he have their blood in him without having a lavish strain of voluptuous life, alike of body and mind.

The Mogul Emperors who took his throne when he could occupy it no more, were men of the same ravishing Eastern school, but not without sentiment in the higher sense, as we find in Shah Jahan's devotion to his Mumtaz and in the wonder of his monument to her. You see the Taj Mahal from the walls of The Fort, as you look across the Jumna, a view the Mogul Emperors, their wives and mistresses, must often have enjoyed. What you see is a spidery wisp of beauty, seeming to float in the air, and guarded by towers at the four corners, " tall court ladies, tending their Princess."

You visit it in the morning when the Indian sun has just risen and is bearable. You return to it at noon, when a blister lies over the Indian earth, leaving only the Taj Mahal cool, like an arum lily. You must be with it when the sun sets, because that is its good-bye, in light and shadow, to the dying day. You cannot, above all, fail to be with it in the moonlight, because then its loveliness is surpassing.

There is something in the Taj Mahal which seems to link the two worlds, ours below and the other, on high, or wherever it may be. It is a romance of two worlds which speaks to you of both, a " house not built with hands," but uprisen from the genii of the East. It inspires, it thrills, it holds the eye and the heart, it fills the whole being, and always it surprises. You think you have captured its shape, its lift to heaven, its grace upon the earth, and you turn away satisfied. But look again, and you find the Taj different, another sort of castle in the air, another creation saying to you in eloquent silence—

"Hold! I am never enough, because I am never the same. A man built me for the sake of a woman, Shah Jahan and his Queen, who lie side by side within me. Man and woman, and God, who made both, are reflected in me, and so I am as romantic as life, as mysterious as death. Nobody ever knows me all, because I am the secrets of the East thrown up to heaven in an essence of beauty which is marble and precious stones, craftsmanship and poetry and always I am—a woman!"

Endless are the moods of the Taj, and they are often contradictory, so, perhaps, suggesting that here we not only have the marble wraith of a glorious woman, but that woman's temperament. Nay, if you will only feel it all rightly, completely, the temperament of Shah Jahan's woman, her very self; aye, and the Eastern beauty and mystery of her presence.

The coolness of the Indian morning finds the Taj warm, like a friend; the fire of noon finds it cool, like a woman's hand laid on a feverish brow;

the retiring sun leaves it fragrant of the ages, hopeful of the future; and the moonlight sanctifies it into a wispish spirit of the earth, because it dwells thereon, but heavenly, because one could not, in all the earth, hope—

To hear a song so clear and strong,
With such a lovely tune.

There is a world-famous architect who visits the Taj Mahal every other year, because he feels it the mother of his art. He learns from it in whispers, and is content to take their echo away with him, knowing he can never hear all there is in the echo it gives back to a voice sent into the silence of its heights. The keepers about the united tomb of Shah Jahan and his beloved cry upward, and the cry returns, silvery and sweet, as if from a paradise where they may now dwell together, in a harmony unbroken by death. For, though we know not whether there be life in death, we do know there is love in death.

Outwardly, in all lights, the Taj is a dream, and inwardly, where incense burns and scents, it is a mystery of beauty and austerity, which is ever the true handmaid of beauty. Moreover, it is perfectly set among trees and grass and water, the jewels of Mother Nature, the great framemaker for human genius. You watch and you pray for a full revelation of this lovely mystery, and, as it comes not, you must be content with your own questions.

What was intended in the Taj Mahal, what was in the thoughts and dreams of those who gave it shape, what messages did they intend it to leave on the mind, the heart, the soul, because it compasses all three? A happy, wonderful accident, a poem in marble, as well as a sepulchre for a kingly Mogul and his queenly and womanly consort?

No; the Taj is too subtle for just that, too finely woven as a thing of lace, too perfect in the relationship of every bit to the other. Devotion and sincerity, earthly affection and a heavenly love must have been at its conception. Soaring artistry, colourful dreaminess, delicate tracery, a high imagination cut in stone and an endless labour, never wearying, never satisfied, must have mingled to build the idea into a monument.

The Taj is remote from the picture of men, has nothing of the characteristics we associate with man, be he Eastern or Western. Here is a woman, a princess of the East, exquisite in spirituality, lovely in the flesh, adorned in robes of shining white, to match the purity of herself. She is veiled, but you can see her face, with its arched eyebrows, its black, languid, praying eyes, its broad, low brow, passing into thick blue-black hair, its Persian nose and Persian creaminess of skin, its seductive, yet spiritual mouth, and its dimpled but grave chin.

Conceive all the loveliness, outward and inward, of the most courtly princess of the East there ever was, translate her into the Taj Mahal, and you begin to know what it is, and how it is what it is. Behold this princess walking in the gardens of her palace, in the splendour of the Indian sun, in the wonder of the moon, or in the light of the stars. Note the exquisite droop of her head, as if she were lost in fond thoughts, listen to the soft rhythm of her footsteps, and then ask yourself, Is she not the Taj Mahal? Is she not the divinity of human life which has given it, marble though it be, the elusiveness of life, the certainty of death, the everything we feel in its presence and cannot say in any words?

We can only wonder, and keep wondering, what mystery of all the worlds and all the gods is enshrined in this architectural jewel of bejewelled India. Mumtaz Mahal lies under a passage of the Koran which says " God is He, besides whom there is no God. He knoweth what is concealed and what is manifest." So it is left to man to keep asking what magic rests in the Taj and is it the spirit of Mumtaz, consecrated by the holy love which bound her and Shah Jahan? For, listen!—

The music of her bangles passed the porch.

IX. WHERE EMPIRES FLAMED

Think, in this batter'd Caravanserai
Whose Doorways are alternate Night and Day,
How Sultan after Sultan with his pomp,
Abode his hour or two, and went his way:
Omar Khayyám.

"IF there be a paradise upon Earth," runs Sa-ullah Khan's famous inscription on the walls of the ancient Diwan-i-Khas at Delhi, "it is this, it is this, it is this!" He was not the first to sing the joys of the Indian spot of earth which became Delhi and has remained so through the rise and fall of seven Delhis.

Go back, with the Hindu epic "Mahabharata," to 1500 B.C., and you may read that here was a region with "Hundreds of palaces and mansions and possessing gates and arches dark as clouds." Moreover, in all this delightful place "There were no robbers, nor any one who was sinful, nor any woman a widow." It was a primitive paradise, not to be found at Delhi to-day, nor anywhere else, because even Paradise is changeable and interchangeable with the centuries.

But Ancient Delhi, which came first, and Old

Delhi, which came next, linger, and New Delhi blooms on the still-living embers of Indian Royalism, as a score of prancing emperors and kings, viceroys and proconsuls practised it. You find a gleam of the old colour at the Viceregal Lodge and in all the ceremonies with which the Viceroy is associated. If it were otherwise, it would seem strange to the people of India, alien to the thread of purple which runs through their inheritance of race and government. Salutation and ceremony, the glitter of scarlet and the flash of gold, the salaam of greeting and the bent knee of obeisance! Those are things that belong to the very life of India, present or past, but at the Viceregal Lodge they are tempered with a personal simplicity which makes them gracious as well as impressive.

Here, as in the guidance of all great affairs, the personality of a Viceroy is much, for he has to hold, by the eye, as well as the heart, a near Indian Kingdom, and by the mind, a distant British Kingdom. There could be no chariot of proconsulship harder to drive, and it merely marks the feat that it is gay with Eastern trappings. Perhaps the Viceroyalty of India, like dancing in the Orient, is best described as dependent on balance and rhythm; certainly, on a wise sense of the practical, qualified by the gift of imagination.

Somehow the old Viceregal Lodge at Delhi does not strike one as an inspiration towards all this, being a scattered place, recruited with emergency tents for guest-quarters. Moreover, while it is inviting in the sense of comfort, and more or less richly furnished, it has no stroke of elegance with which to arrest the visitor. At lunch-time, with the Viceroy in a lounge suit, and his company of guests what it happens to be, the Viceregal Lodge might be mistaken for an English country-house, observing the simple hospitality which we associate with English country life.

But how British character, individual as in a Viceroy, or composite as in him and his staff, impresses itself on the personality of India, even dominates it. You see its natural recognition and easy acceptance in the faces of the fine Indians in fine uniforms, who, with the grave dignity of the Orient and the quiet quickness of a perfect English butler, minister to the Viceroy and his visitors at table. They are masters of ceremony, and they put it, full-handed, at the disposal of the master of affairs, who is the Viceroy. So might the Moguls, when they ruled at Delhi, have been served, but in what a different spirit.

It has always been a natural genius with the British to link old ways with new necessities. You find Old Delhi and New Delhi an immemorial capital of a twentieth century which, East as West, frets with modern fangles in thought, word and

action. One Delhi is a treasury and depository of all time, the other a salute and an assurance to the future. They are separated, thus far, by a mile or two, as they are separated in the ages they personify. But a continuing, binding spirit hovers over them, throwing the same lights and shadows on the crumbled stones as on those quarried to make the new, grander Viceregal Lodge, another page of Indian history, with much, perhaps, to be inscribed upon it.

Is it "love among the ruins" on which all Delhi sits, with white hands and brown hands balancing her reigns of governance between them? Perhaps not, for races sundered in their elements do not readily or generally meet in the intimacy of affection. They keep to their own paths, and "love among the ruins" may—who knows?—not even dwell with everybody in Delhi's English society. Small jealousies are as easily bred as small talk, and official ranking, wherever you meet it on this earth, has a gift for creating both.

Propinquity, somebody has said, is the secret of love, but it may also be a menace of small troubles, especially when the weather is torrid. Then the "single little turret" of official life is apt to preen itself on being a "city great and gay"; and women will be women—thank God! But that's just salt and sincerity, so much diversion for the big side of the Raj in Delhi, between whom and the Indian there does grow a larger sympathy and comprehension. You feel it wherever you go, in private conversation and in public talk, and it is all good manners, which, properly observed, make for definite good feeling. Any bomb-shells, of any sort, in the Parliamentary arena, only emphasise this, just as trouble brings decent people together.

What lamentations may be read in the ancestral stones of Delhi, and yet what messages of hope do they also whisper! There never, perhaps, in all the shaping of mankind was such a bridge-head to build as that which shall link, in body and spirit, the Delhis that have been and the Delhi to be.

"Oh, Prophet," Tamerlane read in the Koran when he launched himself into India, "make war on infidels and unbelievers and treat them with severity." It sounds remote, but the Mohammedans of Delhi, upstanding beside the Hindus, proclaim a modern edge to Tamerlane's sword of the Koran. Convert a people, by force, to a religion, as happened again and again in India, and their far-distant descendants will jealousy defend that religion. So grow and persist religious and racial problems which a Viceroy, seated in his new house, on his old, splendid throne, will have to treat, hand in hand with his Indian Parliament, also given a beautiful meeting house in New Delhi.

Turn the ancient soil on which the Delhis rest, and it will be found rich in historic ores, not easy to group. The Indian sunlight has often been blinding enough to hide deeds of blackness from the personal or the recording eye. The heavenly moonlight has made beautiful things into magic dreams and left them stamped in the very ruins of Delhi. There have been a thousand impossibilities, but they all happened because this is a caravanserai of the Orient.

Stories fill the streets, themselves busy humanly with the many traffics and vehicles of Indian tradition and modern life. Other stories chase you from the narrow alleys and the quaint houses, beseeching to be heard. It is as if you would say that many old Indian shawls are taken out to air, and that you find strange writings woven into them. There is the blood-coloured shawl that a woman of the harem of Persian Nadir Shah may have worn round her shoulders when he sacked Delhi in 1739 and captured the uncanny Koh-i-noor, now one of the Crown Jewels of England. There's a tale for you, with dagger, poison-cup, and bowstring in it, and Delhi, where we are, its scene.

The Koh-i-noor, otherwise the "mountain of light," was a chief trophy of the Mogul Emperors, from Babar onward, and it had illumined the Orient much earlier. Its possession by the Moguls may have excited the cupidity of Nadir Shah, and anyhow the slaughter he wrought enabled him, by a trick, to get it. Sack and carnage went on for a whole day at Delhi, in revenge, said Nadir Shah, for the slaying of his own soldiers. He seized for booty the famous Peacock Throne, the jewels of bejewelled palaces, elephants, camels, and horses. But the Koh-i-noor, which he had intimately in his heart's desire, was missing and could not be found.

There is always an informer in the East, and one came and told Nadir Shah that the great diamond was hidden in the turban of his master, the Mogul Emperor, Mohammed Shah. Slimly, Nadir summoned a durbar, where, such was his courtesy, he reinstated the Mogul on his throne. Nay, as a personal and particular mark of friendship he insisted that they should exchange headdresses. He held out his Persian sheepskin cap to the Emperor, who had to hand his Mogul turban over in exchange, and ruefully he must have done it, knowing that he was also parting with the Koh-i-noor.

It went to Persia, where it blazed on successive Shahs, and eventually it found its way into the jewel-bag of Ranjit Singh, the "Lion of the Punjaub." The "John Company" got it in part payment of the indemnity for the Sikh Wars, and in the 'fifties of last century presented it to young Queen Victoria. What secrets it could tell, of tragedy and romance, of death and love-making, of darkness and dawn in the Orient! More, its story has had its companions in historic

Delhi, while modern Delhi also has plenty of human colour and character.

Mix with educated Indians, and you can study their mentality, evolved by the centuries, and now touched with Western ideas. You discover that the Hindu or the Mohammedan mind is not generally massive, not quick to decide and achieve. It is more the studious mind, patient and careful of detail, such as makes clerks or lawyers, priests or politicians. A reverent mind it can be, for it has browsed on an ancient civilisation, shot with spirituality ; also it can be intellectual, with a subtlety of its own. But this is only to say that here again, the Eastern mind is a natural companion to the more creative, more practical mentality of the West.

Psychology is largely the consequence of climate, and the Briton who has served in Delhi long, knows well the enervating sun. " My children in England, my wife going to the Hills, myself staying in the Plains," said a delightful man, ruefully, about himself. " Shouldn't I," he added, " be had up, or have something done to me, for keeping, not two, but three establishments ? "

There's one of the rubs for the Briton serving India at Delhi or elsewhere, but he goes on with surprising aplomb. His wife may have the grey, drawn lines which Indian " hot weathers " engrave on the fair face of an Englishwoman. Her eyes may be dull, her movements limp, her whole being parchmenty, as if sex had been extracted from it. He, himself, may be so weary with routine work and dusty heat that his natural force and originality are in the prison of convention. But it is "Cheeri-o!" and never about himself, about Delhi, or about India, Omar Khayyám's dark passage:

> *There was a Door to which I found no key,*
> *There was a Veil past which I could not see.*

X. "THE MAN WITH THE HOE"

Bowed by the weight of centuries, he leans
Upon his hoe and gazes on the ground,
The emptiness of ages in his face
And on his back the burden of the world.
Who made him dead to rapture and despair,
A thing that grieves not and that never hopes,
Stolid and stunned, a brother to the ox?

"The Man With The Hoe," by
Edwin Markham.

IT was after he had beheld the "Angelus" and bowed to its unforgettable pathos, that Markham of America wrote his poem. He might, with still greater inspiration and with more direct human message, have written it about the *ryot* of India.

You see him, constantly and endlessly, as you travel its wide plains, a brown, lean, slow-moving figure silhouetted against land and sky, the Indian man of the hoe, though he may own no such implement. This raw tiller of the raw Hindustan soil forms the "masses" of India, constitutes the "people" of India, so let us be at home with him.

You might say that the Great Peninsula is a

continental plain running, with ranges of hills and mountains set in here and there, from Ceylon's spicy isle to the soaring Himalayas. As you travel north, however, you realise that plains can have many varying characteristics in landscape, as well as in human beings. Similarly, the climate varies vastly in different places and even on different days at the same place. Jhansi is said to be the hottest place of British India in the summer, and you can be very hopeless during the time your train halts there.

Somewhere above, a hard, glaring sun, at which you cannot look, except through coloured glasses. A sky blue, but naked of clouds and therefore cruel; nothing anywhere to suggest the gratefulness of shade and shadow—in fine, a wilting world wherever you gaze. If there be an air of wind it is as hot as the breath of a furnace, and you shrink from its suffocation. A fan in the carriage, set to blow on a fading block of ice, struggles to fill your lungs, but only churns up the stew of the atmosphere.

It is the Indian summer, and there is nothing to do but grin and bear it, encouraged, or merely left in wonderment, by the remark, heard somewhere, of a lady whose husband is in the I.C.S. "I have," said she, "stayed with him for nine summers on the plains, and it has just been possible to survive that ordeal." It was the cry of a dutiful and fond wife, of a wounded and

A TYPICAL KASHMIRI GIRL

She is seen at the primitive Kashmir spinning-wheel, wearing, on her winsome person, the scarf, the gown, and the ornaments of her country.

stricken woman, but might she not, out of a larger wisdom, have gone to the Hills? Might he not have been left alone on the Plains, because, the Indian summer apart, an occasional detachment between married people is the keeper of affection.

The Indian *ryot* has no cool "hills" to scale, no sea-breeze, no "home" across the sea and long leave there. He has to get a living from an over-driven soil, and the picture of his doing so suggests to the eye ants on a far-flung flatness. Single dots of human life, here and there, clothed in *pugris* of poor cotton, in jackets of red, or any other colour, and in mere rags for trousers. It is the garb of Old India and the garb for the climate, something at once traditional and cool, but also the badge of penury.

The women of the land clothe themselves in colours of a bolder kind, and wear rings in their ears, their noses, on their fingers, sometimes also on their toes, where, according to an old English ditty, bells should be. This means not only jewellery, but money, in the sense that the baubles have an actual value which the owner could realise in annas and rupees. Certainly to the Indian peasant women, jewels possessed and worn, are money saved, as primitive peoples and Jews have saved it from Bible times onward.

There is quite a jingle when the Indian crowd, gathered at a railway station, bestirs itself as a train approaches or departs. If you were to listen closely enough and long enough, you could almost fancy there was a set melody in the jingle. And the singers might, with their endless variety of colours, be dressed for some great religious service. Unbooted and unshoed feet add to the sense of service, because they make no harsh noise, only a gentle pitter-patter. But there is the crying of many voices selling fruit, offering foods, or inviting the passenger to buy hot or cold water. The passing of a train at an Indian country station is, indeed, an event, and those who attend it might be a small regiment on parade, or the members of a civic reception.

Perhaps somebody, beloved or distinguished, is going away, and he, or she, is, in the pretty Indian manner of " Welcome " or " Good-bye," garlanded with flowers, strings of them placed round the neck. The thoughtful bringers of these flowery tributes may have wetted them well to keep them fresh, and that means clamminess, but you must not know it. There is a good-natured English Sahib who let more wet Indian garlands be hung about his neck than any other man has ever done, and only said, " So pleased ! "

A long whistle goes up from the engine, saying : " Be ready," then a short whistle sounds the start, and you are once more out on the lonely Indian plains, where the sun keeps blazing, and where, in monsoon time, rain will fall like a deluge. Lonely! They must be lonely, for there may not be two little houses in sight at once and there are times when you can see nobody moving, nothing living. Just a dry gully, a ridge of hard, red stone, characteristic of India, or fields divided as minutely as if they were in France, which also has a thick peasant population.

Another time human figures pass in review; a girl drawing water at a well, perhaps an Indian Ruth, in appearance; a woman pounding corn in mortar stones according to the ancient Biblical manner; a man guiding a primitive wooden plough, while a pair of oxen scrape the soil with it for a new crop; a child, brown to almost dark, and oh! so charming in her fragment of covering; or sheep, donkeys, camels, and the animals which compose the flocks and herds, scanty mostly, numerous sometimes, of the *ryot*.

Where there is water there will be birds and wild-fowl crying for something to drink and eat, the double law of all Nature's life. When there are woods, even a few stunted trees, you may catch a glimpse of the gay plumage of a parrot or a cockatoo. Crows, with their croak, make dark spots above the fields and the river-courses, but, when it is hot on the plains of India, you never hear the bird music of England. There is no gaiety in the heat to sing about, only Nature shrinking and shrivelling, but going on, daunted, maybe, yet unquenchable.

No wonder that patience is stamped upon every face, no wonder that in Hindustani there is the saying, " Kuch Parwani "—" Nothing matters." It is resignation, and resignation has an abiding place in the temperament of the Indian, whether he be the plains-man or the hill-man. You can almost watch the elements amid which he spends his days, nights and years, stamping that sign of patience, or rather that brand of patience, upon the weather-worn face of the *ryot*.

The dry earth and the hot sun, the high heavens with the moon and the stars floating in them, are his world, and so himself. His circle of life is his wife and his children—little, sallow-faced things with black, surprised eyes and thin, thin legs—his kine to whatever they may run, and his house which is only a hovel. He sows and he reaps, and if he be a Mohammedan he gets down on a piece of sacking, the nearest thing he can attain to a mat, and says his prayers, and if he be a Hindu he says them in the Hindu way.

He labours for annas, this little Indian *ryot* man, so gentle and so willing, and he is almost wealthy if rupees come his way. With him it is not merely, " Nothing matters," but " What can matter ? " " Salaam " and " Sahib " ! They are his salutations for the world beyond his patch of ground, and he does not ask himself even unconsciously :

How will it be with kingdoms and with kings—
With those who shaped him to the thing he is—
When this dumb Terror shall reply to God
After the silence of the centuries?

A conquered people, the Indian people? Once, perhaps, not now, but subdued, respectful to others and to themselves. All this, qualified by the growing independence of the individual in town and city, for that is chiefly where a new order stirs. The old order of acceptance, taking rule from above and being thankful for it, is restless beside the new education, the new cry, the new spirit. Always, though, the educated, and therefore the articulate Indian, is only one among many who toil dumbly and hope dumbly. That only makes it the more necessary, the more becoming, that the ear of the Raj should hear whispers and understand dreams, especially those of the *ryot*.

XI. THE INDIAN SUN AND MOON

Scent of smoke in the evening,
Smell of rain at night,
The hours, the days and the seasons
Order their souls aright;
Till I make plain the meaning
Of all my thousand years—
Till I fill their hearts with knowledge
While I fill their eyes with tears:
"The Recall," by Rudyard Kipling.

A PILGRIMAGE in India should take you into the market place of human beings, living as best they may, letting live as best they can. It will teach you smells and sores, curses and blessings, beautiful things and ugly things—this blood and flesh, soul and mind bazaar of the Orient. Especially it will teach you that men and women, whether sunburnt until they are brown, or snow-white of skin, have their chief interests in common.

Human nature, wherever you meet it, is very much what it was when people, mostly crusaders and saints, did make real pilgrimages and left us chronicles of them. The ordinary creature is interested in crops and food, in buying and selling, in love, marriage and death, in children, grandchildren, and christenings, and in atoning for sins. Naturally! It is the daily round of life, and it is accompanied by the sun and the moon, gods of sky and earth in India, but oh, such contrasting gods!

Surely the Great God, when he made all things, forgot to temper the Indian sun, which can be crueller than hell itself, because it tortures, without, of necessity, killing. You look out of your window, when the morning is early, and cool and all Nature in India has a fragrance. There are fleecy clouds in the sky and a certain greyness which would in England bespeak a shady day coming. But look deeper into those clouds, and you will see that they only consist of evil portents, that they are a marshalling of terror, camouflaged to look innocent, even quietly beautiful.

Behind a smiling countenance this Jehovah of a sun-god hides a frowning face, and he means to get you. Slowly his torch burns, then it bursts into full flame, and the ramparts of cloud which had promised to stand between it and you vanish. The blaze launches at you, red and burning, and you know that no chance will interfere with its conquest of you and the day. A thunderstorm! Perhaps! It needs time to gather, and when it has done that it will happen somewhere, very locally, most likely. The sun, itself, is universal, the fire of India as well as the light of the whole wide world.

Our English sun is like a cheerful friend risen from his bed to offer us a good morning and assure us of a good day. The Indian sun is an enemy who has lain in ambuscade for us all night, as a beast waits in the jungle for its prey in the morning. He prepares his spring, seizes his victim by the head, the face, the eyes, by his whole being, and holds him there in suppliant and tortured fee. Oh! Indian sun, how cruel you can be to animals and children, to grown-ups of both sexes, to everything we call life, and when you sink into your den at eventide you leave the earth sweltering.

Perspire, perspire, perspire! It is a melting business, and it never ceases in the high noon of the Indian summer. "Have I come through?" you often ask, and are asked, in the day-time. You go to bed exhausted, and when you open your eyes in the morning, not from a refreshing sleep, but from a restless doze, you will see a shadow on the sheet, and it seems very like your shadow. So it is: the shadow of the night done in perspiration; a sweat-o-graph.

It makes you think of the old tombs of knights and esquires, topped with effigies of the warriors resting below. You also have been in a hot campaign, and this is your token of it; you have printed yourself on a winding-sheet, and you will

SUNRISE IN FAIR KASHMIR

The silken Jhelum River, with a native doonga drifting idly down-stream, and a new day coming up from the Himalayas

do it again next night, while you toss and tumble and for coolness sigh to yourself:

Here we go, in a flung festoon,
Half-way up to the jealous moon.

Curiously gentle is the Indian moon, as if it sought to atone for the cruelty of its partner of the day. It comes up with a timorous, halting gait, as much as to say, " Will you permit me ? " It has a warm, rosy bashfulness, with a soft laugh behind the warmth, and it would wink to you if you gave it the least encouragement. This friendly face grows in its blessing, as the darkness falls like a dark curtain on India, and then it is the benign sovereign of the Heavens.

What ruddy cheeks the moon-man has, and what a jolly night he and you are going to have! Perhaps he knows Byron and the line about the devil being in the moon, but he means to be a nice devil. Such a good-natured moon! Such a whimsical moon! A Christmassy and good-cheer sort of moon, friendly towards all mankind all womenkind, star-gazers and moonshiners included.

" My colleague, the sun," he whispers across space, " has given you a savage day, but he is a hard fellow. Trust me to give you a gentle night, a night of elfin light; not glaring daylight made into a savage mirage, but evening cloaked and clothed in velvet; a twilight of sensuous beauty which opens the heart and comforts it, which inspires the mind and consoles it, which stirs the blood and satisfies it!"

The Indian moon speaks to you so, though you may not always hear him, for his whisper is a small voice in the wilderness of the sky. Still he speaks often to those who understand him, and he has a message for them, especially for lovers who have met in the glamour of the Indian Ocean, or the witchery of the Indian heat, and know what to say to each other. He holds them by their hands and leads them, but they must take care, because the Indian moon has a way which is dangerous.

It says, in its flirtation half-lights, "Come"; and then it says, "You see where you have come," and adds, "Beware, for I am the Indian moon, which no man or woman resists for long." Yes, and—

Whom once the moon has kissed, loves long and late,
Yet never finds the maid to be his mate.

But this Indian moon has lights and shadows which transfigure valleys where it is very, very pleasant to wander: valleys of allure, with songs calling from hills, with rest-houses and temples for those who would tarry by the way. A very perfect lantern of sentiment is the Indian moon at night-time, when Mother Nature is most generous with her blandishments. She flings them broadcast upon the waters of the ocean, where they shimmer like a Sultana's necklace of diamonds. She throws them to the distant Southern Cross, and catches them as they fall down again in sprays of exquisite glitter.

Silver shines in the Indian moon, showing its cousinship to our orb of a more western, more northern heaven. But its face and its heart are golden, and therefore its being is golden, kindly, friendly. It is the good companion and philosopher of everybody who cares to explore the glories and the mysteries of the Indian night.

You can keep in that heaven of exploration wherever you travel, from Bombay to Burma, or from Madras to Kashmir, taking in Calcutta on the way. Trains in India travel far and fast, and in the summer, everything is done to meet the heat; a shower-bath for the wealthy traveller, windows of smoke-glass to keep out the glare, large, roomy compartments so that there may be an atmosphere in which to live and breathe. Yourself, you breakfast and lunch and dine in the restaurant-car, so meeting your fellow-travellers sociably and perhaps learning a few "Dont's" for India.

Don't drink any water unless it has been boiled, and you can always get minerals of some kind. There is a tale of a lady who even brushed her teeth with soda-water and certainly they were pretty teeth. Don't eat natural fruits, of which there are many, unless they have been washed, or you know from whose garden they have come.

"Dont's" of the merely advisory sort also come in, for there are times when Tropic risks are greater than at other times, and it is just as well to discover them and bear them in mind. Don't drink a "chota peg" of Scotch and soda or any peg with spirits in it, before sundown. It is the constant advice you will get in India, and whether it be necessary advice or merely good advice, you had better follow it. Maybe its chief wisdom lies in the fact that it is a health order, like the laws of Moses, the orders of Mohammed, and half the wisdom of all the wise religious teachers. Anyhow, on a railway journey it is best to avoid all spirits during the day, and to touch only such drinks as ginger-beer, given snap, perhaps, by anointment with a little gin.

Europeans in India have lots of wonderful drinks, and nothing better, perhaps, as an appetiser than a "gimlet." Its chief ingredients are gin and lime-juice, and it bores itself into you in a most cool and agreeable fashion. "Not so dusty," said an English visitor when he was introduced to it, and his remark would have been expressive in another sense if that "gimlet" had found its destiny during a long railway journey in the Indian summer time.

But India has a winter which is all an English summer, a real June-time, and then travel is not only a luxury but a joy. A cool air tempers the Oriental sun in the day, and, in the northern parts, this may mean wood fires at night. Travel then and rugs and blankets are the order; so it is India from October to March and on to Kashmir for the spring. This wise you will find "sweetness and light," most grateful to life, and never be away from the testimony, in song, which the bulbul and other Indian birds pay to a delightful season. They also sing in "the rains" which cool the land and make it green, for the South West Monsoon, on one side, and the Bengal Monsoon on the other side, are, with the snowy Himalayas, the saviours of Hindustan.

You meet with adventures while you travel in India—not anything serious, unless you ask for it, but fresh, revealing experiences. For instance, the *chaukidar;* a big, picturesque fellow, scion and son, no doubt, of the ancient hill-men of India, and now in service as, in plain terms, a night watchman. He marches round your hotel at night, armed with a spear which is at once his badge of office and his means of defence. A bear? Not likely. A hyena? Perhaps. A pie-dog? Quite possibly. A thief? Certainly, if he is not afraid to come.

A spearman I met particularly, in the glimpses of the Indian moon at Rawalpindi, liked his job, and capered now and then with his weapon, as if he wanted to use it. The compound was all golden, and the sharp, cruel whistle of the mosquito was in the air which rustled the leaves. Here and there a figure moved irregularly, dreamily—native servants of the hotel finding their sleeping quarters, others sleeping on the grass in all sorts of corners—and away, in the distance, a European woman, as you could tell by her short skirts, exercising her dog. Altogether a good night for a spearman, a mighty good night, but what he said was merely "Salaam," and the mosquito curtain of my bungalow bedroom answered " Salaam," and I went behind it.

What a capital way they have of planning hotels in India: a central building where you eat, meet each other, and live generally, and streets of bedrooms around it. You have mine host, but you also have your freedom, and one could weave romance out of the possibilities of that freedom. Actually, the architects of Indian hotels have no thoughts of the sort; simply, ground is plentiful and cheap, servants can be had for very small wages, and the heat is not to be closed in on people. Romance thereupon gives place to utility and habit, and they become convention, which keeps us all safe from—

The moon's dark disc in her crescent pale.

XII. HILLS AND A HAPPY VALLEY

Then I felt like some watcher of the skies
When a new planet swims into his ken ;
Or like stout Cortez when with eagle eyes
He star'd at the Pacific—and all his men
Look'd at each other with a wild surmise—
Silent, upon a peak in Darien.

"On First Looking into Chapman's Homer," by Keats.

A LONG darkish blur in the sun-lit atmosphere, then a bluish wall rising from nowhere, and finally rugged shapes topped with white. Nobody is ever likely to forget a first sight of the Himalayas, as they look down on India, for a world of great mountains is even more impressive than a sea of great waters.

We had, hours before, bidden good-bye to Lahore and its thirteen gates, a citadel of old time and now, of India on the flat. It might have held us for a week, and then not have parted with half the history in its stones, half the personality in its sacred and secular places. But hope, on a journey, ever steers north, and there, far and clear, were the Himalayas with, hidden in their folds, a wonder-road to the wonder-land of Kashmir.

You leave the Frontier Mail at Rawalpindi, called for short " Pindi," which is a postern of the North-west Frontier, with Peshawar further on, then the Khyber Pass, and after that Afghanistan and No-Man's-Land. It is roughly two hundred miles from " Pindi " to Srinagar, but to-day they are done by motor-car, whereas not so very long ago they had to be done by *tonga*, the pony trap which is common to India, and comfortable enough when you do not get too much of it.

It's a breakneck business, the road to Srinagar, but, for its adventure and splendour, it is also the journey of a life-time. You can do it in a day, only the best thing is to stay the night at some dak-bungalow, a natively kept rest-house, of which there is a series for the traveller. Camels, cows, donkeys, horses, picturesque people —all the elements of traffic into " Pindi " are soon left behind. You rise steadily and constantly, as the growing coolness of the air assures you. Wisely you have changed into warm clothes, for there is as much difference between the temperature of Kashmir and India as there is between London and Sicily. Tweeds and woollies, such as we use at home, are what you want in the high land of Kashmir, except during the warmest months of summer, June, July and August.

A KINGDOM FOR POETS

Beyond, the Himalayas; near by, Solomon's Throne and, below, the Jhelum at Srinagar, with the braiding house-boats of English folk.

At Murree, the first stage on the journey from "Pindi," you are eight thousand feet up in the clouds, and you feel the cold in your bones. How delicious after the swelter of the Indian Plains, and yet how shivery, for the human body cries out about the least inconvenience, being a selfish organism. But we are threading our way into the heart of the Himalayas, along the banks of the Jhelum River, and what would you expect but a crisp air?

We never lose sight of the Jhelum for more than a few moments, and sometimes the road seems to hang over it, sometimes even to be tumbling into it. Big, brownish-yellow, full with the ever-melting, never-ending snows of the Himalayas, it roars down upon us, hurrying away to the thirsty places of India. The noise of its great waters, kept bottle-necked by many gorges, comes to our ears like the tune of an organ played by a god, for hardly anywhere in its descent, as rapid as our ascent, is there enough level ground for a pool.

Such has been our passage to Murree, from which we plane swiftly down towards the Vale of Kashmir proper, and at Kohala we rest from darkness until daylight next morning. Cars and carriages are not allowed to travel at night on this Himalayan highway, unless in an emergency, for that would be to court accidents and to have encounters with the bullock-carts of native traffic.

They have the road to themselves at night, and they crawl along as if their day's bivouac by the wayside, in favour of the fast traffic, had still left them half asleep.

Our dak-bungalow is elementary but enough, and indeed it is surprising how simple one can be when simplicity is the iron order of things. My quarters are a large room like a small coach-house, with a double-winged door and a modest window in front, and behind a kind of passage-way opening out on to heights which seem dark and mysterious. A little enquiring walk around the framework which stands for a bed, because in India a traveller carries his own bedding; a wooden fire which cracks merrily up the open fireplace; a meal which is plain but good, and, as Pepys would have said, perhaps even in Kashmir, " So to bed."

Never a dream by a mind drugged with many sights, never a movement of a body weary after long travels. Sweet oblivion, until the dark is passing to the dawn, and in the haze between the two, my Indian bearer—a personal servant half-valet, half-courier—Kewal Ram, puts a lighted candle and a pot of tea on the trestle table in the room. He has also captured an orange, the friend of every parched traveller in India, and, what is still more welcome, enough hot water for a shave.

Soon our chauffeur, a dark Sikh, a noticeably

graceful fellow with small bones, delicate hands, and a brain like a shot, can be heard tuning up his engine. He has slept in the car all night, soundly, one judges, beside the rumble of the Jhelum, for he is as fresh, as alert, as trig as you like. Off we go again, and if the evening on the road to Kashmir had been memorable, the morning is twice wonderful.

We had seen the mighty Himalayas, as, with white night-caps on their heads, they awaited the heavy Indian darkness. A setting sun braided them with flashes of gold and splashes of violet, with spangles of smoke-blue and ribbons of fire-red, with a whole gallery of coloured good-nights. It is a revelation, the wealth of colours which Indian Mother Nature has in her brush, and it is nearly as lavish when she goes to bed as when she leaves it.

Now the sun of a new day is unveiling a hundred Himalayan peaks as if they were timorous maidens in virgin white going to a first sacrament. Wherever one looks, there are minarets of snow, suffused with pink, shot with saffron, streaked with blue, illumined with ever so many hues, like an ancient manuscript, and Mother Nature's writing on the Himalayas is terribly old. There they rise, eternal, immutable, the same yesterday, to-day, and to-morrow, and yet always different, for the personality of mountains changes, as if they were alive, elegant men, graceful women.

Every mile we cover—and, for all the seeming hazard, we take them most quickly—the Himalayas are a fresh revelation, the Happy Valley of Kashmir, nestling under them, a fresh field of loveliness. It charms and they fascinate, as—

> *Wide-spread they stand . . . .*
> *Ancient, mysterious, brooding savage dreams.*

Here a sheer precipice runs up from the Jhelum, as far as the eye will go without tiring in the brilliant light. This precipice, as you see in more detail through your smoked spectacles, is clothed from the water-edge with flowers and shrubs and trees, which bloom in so many shades that they make a huge peacock's tail, with even the little eyes blinking at each other.

Another time the hills on our side of the Jhelum sweep grandly down to its broad ribbon of water, grasping, as if to prevent them falling, a bundle of little houses, whose habitants are working in the fields. Bony cows are grazing all about, sheep are nibbling the pasturage, and generally the animals which are vegetarian are afoot in this ancient, though to us, new Land of Promise.

They have no difficult quest, because, when the Gods of India made it, they began with snow and ice on the northern heights, and these, melting into many waters, irrigate Kashmir beyond all exhaustion. What a generous dowery! Springs and streams cool to drink from, an ice-cold shock to put your hand in; and, on the other hand, a mid-day sun which has both a fine heat and a fine gaiety. That bespeaks an atmosphere in which it is a sheer joy to travel, and we are almost grieved to pass strings of Kashmiris on the march, some of them returning from a winter's work in the Punjaub, or a group of women and children come forth bashfully from their elementary homes, to see strangers.

It means that our motor-car journey, far though two hundred miles had seemed, is always getting nearer its end, and indeed the Jhelum tells us this. For at Baramula it has ceased to be a torrent, hurrying away south, and has become a broad, quiet stream, with quaint craft on its bosom, an easy-going and opulent river, most content to water the levels of Kashmir. Swift anger is no more its portion, but, instead, a sweet smoothness, a gentle leisure, which call you to linger on its banks, all contentment.

Somehow, in this form and mood, it makes one think of our own English Thames, drifting down the pleasant landscape which lies between Oxford and Windsor. But the Thames is small and sweet, while the Jhelum is mighty in volume and mightily set among the lordliest mountains of the earth. If you like, though, you can suppose the Thames Valley, in its physical and spiritual appeal, to be a pocket edition of the Jhelum Valley, and then let your imagination do the rest, without fearing, in the least, that it will be overdone.

Here is majesty crowned by the heavens, clad in a rich greenery which, all the summer, climbs towards the snow-line, and based on a garden of many miles and endless beauty. First impressions are necessary generalities, as when you look into a face and are just taken by its whole aspect. But the instinct behind first impressions is mostly right, certainly a woman's instincts, and ours as to the Vale of Kashmir are already definite.

They overflow when we come into the wide, soft shade of the poplars which line the roads around Srinagar, its historic, picturesque capital. Those slender, lifting trees came to Kashmir with the Persians or with some other invaders, and they have become a common feature of the country. They are as tall land-ships in a country of waters, and their gentleness of bearing, notwithstanding their stature, is characteristic of Kashmir.

You divine it to be kindly, even while you are only making an arrival salaam to its outward beauty. Confirmation will come, with future discoveries and surprises, and meanwhile we are only a mile from our hearts' desire, a beautiful English home looking up to the Himalayas and out upon the Jhelum river. Ah! and a lovely garden in which to dream with "Paradise Lost," of Paradise Found in a—

Sweet interchange
Of hill and valley, rivers, woods and plains.

XIII. A LAND OF SPLENDOURS

Cashmere still maintains its celebrity as the most delicious spot in Asia or in the world.

Elphinstone's " India."

I touch my brow, as the Easterners do ;
May the Peace of Allah abide with you.

An Indian Salaam.

IT is a fine morning, restful and zestful, after much travel, and here we are in the bosom of fabled Kashmir. Let us go forth and look at it with eye and mind and heart, seeking for the things which will only come at leisure. They are all there, but, like fairies, they refuse, at first, to reveal more than their presence, and have to be courted. You can see, at a glance, what a landscape is like, but you must live with it if you are to understand it and enjoy it, as you would a dear friend.

A wise way of gaining the confidence of a country is to stand " tip-toe upon a little hill " overlooking it, and the Takht-i-Suleiman, or Throne of Solomon, is here, beckoning us. It rises, a thousand feet high or so, above the Jhelum, as that river winds down from the great eminences

THE MIGHTY HIMALAYAS

Nanga Parbat, the fourth highest mountain in the world, as it looks down on Kashmir, whose people call it the "Home of the Gods."

upon Srinagar, and it has an old religious shrine for a cap. This pious shrine was there, in some shape, when the calendar of time only pointed at 200 B.C., and it has many traditions of visiting Buddhists and wandering Llamas from Tibet. One concerns a fakir who lived in it, called himself water-carrier to King Solomon, and descended the hill every day for a supply to the Dal Lake, dancing below.

At night a light, symbol always and everywhere of eternal life, shines from the shrine on the "Takht," as, for short, not too-reverent people call King Solomon's Throne. But now the morning glows, though not yet hotly, as it will a little later. The air has a fresh life, as of a new birth, and as of a traveller who says to himself: "A good start, at a lovely dawn, makes amends for all the evils of yesterday." A gentle movement of atmosphere, rather than a breeze, caresses the "Takht," for, though you are above the Vale of Kashmir, you are still within its sheltering fold.

Look! And look again! Still the wonder grows, and when it fills you full, much will be left for others. You are, turn what way you will, confronted with scenes which explain why a Kashmiri, perhaps without knowing it, "Sees God in clouds and hears him in the wind." Eden lies down there where the Jhelum winds a pattern that ran into the old Kashmir shawl, and is strangely similar to the pattern of the old Paisley shawl, just as the lotus appears constantly in Kashmir embroidery. It is an Eden, fragrant with the scent of flowers, melodious with the song of birds, and that, you feel, touched by the reverence of the Buddhist shrine, must have been ordained.

But to the Kashmiris, at their small, daily round and their laborious daily task, God in Heaven may seem far away, very remote, because He is above the Himalayas, and they lose themselves in the clouds. Nanga Parbat is traditionally the "home of the Gods," and it is nearly 27,000 feet in height, the fourth giant of the world, so incredibly high that to your eye it seems the mirage of a snow-mountain drifting in the sky.

It remains, like Mount Everest, the father of the Himalayas, unconquered by man, though, no doubt, it will be scaled one fine day, because man constantly triumphs over Nature, whether or not it be always worth while. You cannot see Nanga Parbat from the "Takht," but away to the left, a barrier between Kashmir and the Punjaub, there challenges the famous Pir Panjal Range, "whose snowy ridge the roving Tartar bounds."

Here, most surely, is a land of "mountain and flood," for they are not only everywhere, but they make it a picture of beauty. There was an Indian sultan who named a river "The

Eye's Repose," and he might have so named the outspreading Vale of Kashmir. When Jehangir the Mogul was dying, he said he wanted "Only Kashmir; I want nothing else," because it was engraved on his heart. He would have known the "Takht," since hills have always been, and he would have remembered longingly that—

Summer, in a vale of flowers,
Lay sleeping rosy at its feet.

That is the general picture looking from Solomon's Throne, but when you bid your eye search for detail, you discover many and various elements. Srinagar, the "City of the Sun," holding long and tightly to either bank of the Jhelum and then scattering back into the country landscape. The Jhelum itself, carrying the town on its broad, cool bosom, nourishing as any mother's, East or West, for this, mind you, is the Venice of India, with its canals to prove that. Ancient temples, old mosques, green, because garden-roofed houses, open-windowed shops, gable-ended buildings of a nondescript kind, with native craft flecking the face of the waters and, here and there, "Places of nestling green for poets made."

Next the eye goes out to the lush plain which enframes town and river; its damp rice-fields, its grazing kine, and its general aspect of Nature in motherly bloom, however small or great may be the crop gathered from her arms. Away in the distance is the Wuler Lake, restful in the sun, but, remembering the near Himalayas, capable of strange and tragic storms. Hence you ask—

Is this the lake, the cradle of the storms,
Where silence never tames the mountain war?

Tempest is hard to fancy, with the Dal Lake laughing and the old Mogul pleasure-gardens smiling back, but Nanga Parbat and the Sindh Valley know better. They are not, however, candid, not confiding, like the gun which daily proclaims the noon hour from Akbar's Fort, the time-keeper of Kashmir, on the hill of Huri Parbat.

You like to fancy while you hear the shot roll up and down the valley and lose its voice in the far heights, that you see the poplar trees of Srinagar unbend in a salaam. How elegantly they could do it, stiff, upright, proud as they look, lining yonder road or this near avenue, for they are a true inset of the landscape. Possibly they were first planted to shelter the summer traveller from the sun and the winter traveller from the cold blast of the Himalayas. They leap upward, long stalks with silver-grey bark, shadowing the pools of water which jewel the rice-fields in the spring. They are there, sorrier looking but enduring, when the heat comes to parch Kashmir's greenery into rose-pink, scarlet, or bronze, according to the fashion of the season.

She has, like a beautiful, well-dressed woman, a whole wardrobe of colours : soft blues, exquisite greens, delicate violets, pale roses, warm indigoes, and rich golds. The Indian sky is her cloak, and the Himalayas hang it round her, and the Jhelum is her bath and her silver slippers. And she is beautifully shaped, as a woman should be, if she is to wear her clothes in that Eastern way which teases, with inward mystery, while it charms with outward grace.

You should understand that the Vale of Kashmir, strictly defined, is a verdant plain nearly a hundred miles long, and up to twenty-five miles broad. It stands more than five thousand feet above sea level, and might, with fancy and truth, be called the Riviera of Asia. But it is among grander surroundings than the Riviera of Europe, nestling between the Mediterranean and the Alpes Maritimes. Both are traps for the sun, and if the Indian sun can be a blazer, why, the Himalayas cool him down for Kashmir, unless at his midsummer rampage.

But what Elphinstone wrote of Old Cashmere remains true—that " It is placed, by its elevation, above the reach of the heat of Hindustan, and, sheltered by the surrounding mountains from the blasts of the higher regions, it enjoys a delicious climate, and exhibits, in the midst of snowy summits, a scene of continual verdure and almost perpetual spring."

"Oh, to be in Kashmir, now that April's there"! One might well say that, as Browning said it about England, for April is a perfect month in the Himalayan Valley. A green land, rushing waters, a golden sun, all inspiration for body and mind, soul and heart. Come September, and it brings coolness again, and gives dale and hill a wealth of bewitching colour, which winter will, in due course, change into a robe of crystal sunshine in the sky and much snow on the Himalayas.

There is always snow on them, and from your view-point on the "Takht" you may, so fine and far is vision, see the pranks of a Himalayan storm any morning, afternoon, or evening. At your feet are stretches of flowering, quivering mustard and streaks of grey willows, misty and elusive; while afar, on the unmeasured heights, a snow-storm rages. It prances and capers, a mad, violent thing, and if you put your hand to your ear you may hear echoes as of a rushing, mighty wind. Fantastic shapes scamper across the mountains, rainbows play about the peaks, and high, high up, there shoots an uncanny yellow streak, token of angry lightning.

Splendour of immensity, stupendousness of desolation, sights which suggest death and birth at the same time in a world crowned, and so fathered by the god-like Himalayas! Sight and thought atop Solomon's Throne fill you with all that majesty, and you are glad to turn downward to the soft, velvety savanna of the Jhelum, where there are roses, roses all the way. You linger by a deodar, remembering that the luxurious Moguls used the wood of this tree to heat a bath, because of its wonderful perfume, which, like the Vale of Kashmir—

Could melt the coldness of a maid, the sternness of a saint.

XIV. SWEETHEART OF THE WORLD

The sailor plucked an apple from an orchard, as he passed,
On a bright October morning that brought him home at last,
And, as he munched he muttered—"Why can't I always be
Where a lad can pluck an apple from an overhanging tree?"

Wilfrid Gibson.

ALWAYS Kashmir has been the world's sweetheart of countries, a real Land of Promise to mankind seeking beauty and romance, an undying quest. Always its bright allure has lighted the sombre earth, a lamp set in a high place. So it has gathered tradition and history, and in the mists of the one and the folds of the other, we have a story which can be heard at leisure. For we easily "fall," as the American word is, and as the word may well be here, to that characteristic of the Kashmiris.

Simple people! Do they reflect that Alexander the Great passed here, leaving behind him enough Greek soldiers to assure Kashmiri women of lovely profiles and, often, white skins? He embarked

As in a Glass—
Clearly!

On the banks of the Dal Lake, whose silvery, dreamy waters make shadows into realities.

on the Jhelum, so we may read, in order to get to the Indus, but that red thread of olden time is elusive.

Akbar and the other Mogul kings loved and lorded the Vale of Kashmir centuries after " windy Troy " had flamed " for a woman's golden head." " The chief of the kings of the world, Shah Akbar," was an inscription this particular Mogul left on a mountain ; " may his dominions extend." The Emperor Babar, in his memories, links an ancient race of the Upper Sindh, the Kâs, with the possible origin of the name Kashmir, but that, also, is another mystery of the Happy Valley.

Its position, in the very heart of the great continent we call Asia, made it familiar, though remote. Good tidings of its climate, its verdancy, its women, and its wine, were as a calling wind in the very deserts of Central Asia. It was overrun by every warlike race in turn—Tartars, Tibetans, Moguls, Afghans, Pathans, Sikhs—who all left footprints in its sands of history. But the Kashmiris themselves just went on, accepting conqueror after conqueror, and so drifting down the stream of time, perhaps because the silken lotus of the Dal Lake infected them. They were shaped hewers of wood, drawers of water, tillers of the soil, and cunning craftsmen in various arts, not stout fellows in armour.

Whole pages of Eastern colour fall open to the

touch of one's imagination, let loose on the spot. There was a Raja, a Shah, or a King of Kashmir when the world was as young as 500 B.C. Of another Kashmir ancient there lingers the saying, so eloquent of a "pot and gallows" age, that "One caldron and one fire saw seven kings before the flesh was boiled." They must have followed each other quickly into hot water, but, then, Eastern kingship was ever a precarious business. No doubt the gamble was worth while, for there is legend of a royal adventurer in Kashmir who had "nine hundred thousand foot, three hundred elephants, and a hundred thousand horse." He also is dim, and he may even be doubtful, for the date of him is the ninth century A.D., but he illustrates the blazonry which braids Kashmir.

Beyond, when there were no milestones, only empty darkness, lies the tradition of how the vale turned into that, from being a huge Himalayan lake. A demon, or Jala, a sort of spirit god, who preyed upon primitive Kashmir mankind and womankind, had his home and fastness among these deep waters. A holy man came on the scene, living piously, and then, when he heard of the demon, austerely, because he was gathering moral forces for his destruction. The Great God heard the saint's prayers, and sent Vishnu and Brahma to destroy the monster, which they eventually did, by opening the Himalayas at Baramula, because he was thus left to flounder on dry land,

and could be slain. Does it not suggest the legend of our St. George and the Dragon, with differences in the telling?

How plain the childhood of the world would be without its faint, tracery-like traditions, because they are as varied as the flowers on a Kashmir *karewah*. It is a flat-topped, dwarfish eminence that you find scattered about in the valley, always, you are told, a relic of the original bottom of the lake in which—shall we assume?—the demon Jala dwelt. Anyhow, the bed of the valley is much lower than the bed of the lake would have been, and as the *karewahs* are, with their crops of rice and corn, for they are fertile under the bullock-plough of the Kashmiri *ryot*.

What thoughts does he croon while, bare-legged, bare-footed, and thinly clad elsewhere, he trudges across the sludgy-widgy haughs, as patient and laborious as his oxen? If he be a Mohammedan, he may say that it was really the Prophet Suleiman who drained Kashmir of its lake waters, not Vishnu and Brahma. Or did those mighty waters simply burst the Himalayas without help from any holy man, Hindu or Mohammedan? Perhaps the Kashmir *ryot* has none of these speculations, for they do not concern his humble daily round. And he will be without knowledge of a nearer subject—how Kuta Rani, a soldier's daughter, raised an army when, in the fourteenth century, the last of the Hindu sovereigns of Kashmir fled before some new conqueror. A salute goes to her heroism and a tear falls for her fate, because she stabbed herself to avoid an unwelcome marriage.

Onward with the clock of history until the year 1819, which is modern beside the age of Kashmir, and recent against the background of the Himalayas. Ranjit Singh and his victorious generals entered the valley then, for the bold Sikhs took it from the brave Pathans, while we were settling up our Waterloo victory. It became part of the Sikh Punjaub, and remained Sikh until the end of the Sutlej Campaign, when we occupied Lahore and, by doing so, also acquired Kashmir.

You see, we did have this Garden of Eden in the hollow of our hands, ours not only to have, but to hold. " Kashmir," an English traveller wrote, " will become the focus of Asiatic civilisation, a miniature England in the heart of Asia." He was prophesying what might have happened, but better than events bore out, for what actually happened ?

Sir Hari Singh's forbear, the old, roguish, far-planning Gulab Singh, was the Maharaja of Jammu on the southern edge of the Himalayas, and of it only. He was the chief of a Hindu family in a little kingdom which, to-day, is evenly divided between Hindus and Mohammedans, while Kashmir, notwithstanding the religion of its ruler is about three parts Mohammedan. Curious, one repeats, the hammering, by force, of an Indian people from faith to faith and then, when the conversion has become complete, their refusal of influences which would carry them back where they were. Perhaps the Prophet of Islam was not so far wrong when he made the sword the text of his religion, certainly among Orientals.

It is cynical to say that religion is also custom, but, anyhow, Gulab Singh, a Dogra by race, had helped us in our conflict with the Sikhs, and in token of this we made him what was almost a present of Kashmir. Strictly recorded, the pact, dated March the 16th, 1846, in the reign of Queen Victoria, was, that he paid us for Kashmir, seventy-five lacs of rupees, or less than half a million sterling. Also he came to our assistance with his whole army—such as it might be—if we fell into war with any people near his frontier. Further, he gave us entrance to Kashmir and kept open roadway for us through its territory. Finally, he acknowledged our full supremacy, including the management of all Kashmir's relationships with other Indian States; and, of course, its further relationships are with the Viceroy of India. The continual evidence of all this was that the Maharajas of Kashmir should, every year, send the British sovereign half a dozen of the famed Kashmir shawls.

We had so much to do in India about the middle of last century, first as the "John Company," and then as England, that we were probably glad to provide for the Himalayan kingdom in this fashion. But it was a splendid deal for Gulab Singh, and no wonder his present successor is careful that the Kashmir shawls coming annually to Buckingham Palace, shall be the very finest, beautiful Eastern wraps for beautiful Western shoulders. They represent a loyal salute and a gallant gesture, but what are they against the heavenly Vale of Kashmir and all the hill country around it, even mysterious Ladakh?

The Himalayan kingdom which thus came to Gulab Singh was promptly got in hand by him, and, according to all accounts, he was a man who ruled with an iron hand, loving power in reality, as well as in circumstance. "The courtyard of the palace at Jammu," we have a contemporary record, "was alive with crowds of officers and attendants, gorgeously apparelled in red and yellow shawls, and armed with spears, swords, and match-locks." There was a bit of a revolt among Gulab's subjects, and, we have it, "Some of his prisoners were flayed alive under his own eye. The executioner hesitated, and Gulab Singh asked him if he were about to operate upon his father or mother, and rated him for being so chicken-hearted." A thorough-going raja, evidently, and yet a fellow of humour, for when a pious Sikh complained about the noise of a Mullah calling his flock to prayer, he answered, "Very well; if you'll collect the flock for him I'll order him to be silent."

Gulab must have been too complete an autocrat to base himself upon a one-time Sikh Governor of Kashmir, who at breakfast ate largely of almonds stewed in butter, and never, by any chance, went to bed sober. No doubt in his time the valley was " all love and light, visions by day and feasts by night." To-day things are different, and the hand of the average Indian maharaja, or raja—great raja or little raja—is at least velvet-gloved.

At Kashmir or at Jammu there is no great State ceremony, but, in an India being cast for modern ways, they keep all their ancient repute and gallantry. As witness of that, Kashmir may, some day, yield the women of the world such emeralds that their own beauty will be in danger of eclipse. They will risk that, and thus the glory which has been Kashmir will once more be justified, as in Indian poetry of the past, for—

Thereat the Ranee, Neila, unbraided from her hair
The pearls as great as Kashmir grapes, Soorj gave
his wife to wear ;
And all across her bosom, like lotus-buds to see,
She wrapped the tinselled sari of a dancing Kunchenee.

XV. HOW THE JHELUM FLOWS

The line of beauty was never more faithfully depicted in landscape than by the course of the broad and beautiful Jhelum, the "fabulous Hydaspes" of the Augustan Age. So regular, without being too much so, are its windings as it approaches the city (of Srinagar) from the southward; so just are the length and curvature of its sweeps, and so well-proportioned are its width and the space it occupies, to the extent of the rich savannah through which it flows; so tranquil and lake-like is the surface of the water, that, at first, we cannot divest ourselves of the idea that nature has called in the assistance of art and has ornamented the scenery beneath us with reference to the most approved principles of landscape gardening.

Vigne's "Travels in Kashmir."

GREAT rivers are like the veins in a face, for they not only irrigate and nourish, but give colour and expression. They are, in both cases, a tidal life-blood, for the Mother of all works on one wonderful, wonderfully simple plan. She fashions us and our surroundings, and then, looking on in irony or in pity, lets us scratch the surface of things, until we get down far enough for a grave.

Old Vigne, when he wandered in Kashmir long

A Stream of

The long, graceful windings of the Jhelum, as

years ago, perceived that the Jhelum River was a jewel in the casket of Mother Nature. The country was then utterly remote, a traditional oasis lost in the grandeur of the Himalayas, rather than an appurtenance of the white man's world. It was the Hindu Kush to him, but the Jhelum River was the same as now, or almost the same.

What is it if engineers make its banks into a high bund at Srinagar, partly for traffic purposes, chiefly to keep it from flowing over into floods? Merely it goes on gathering silt, thus lifting its bed stealthily inch by inch, until, one day, when the mighty waters from the Himalayas are mightier than usual, and over the top of the bund they burst, satiric Mother Nature!

You may harness the Jhelum stoutly, but, always, it has to be regarded with imagination, because it has temperament, which, in a river, or a landscape, becomes atmosphere, something almost personal. You cannot abide by the banks of the Jhelum, or cruise on its waters, without feeling this in your body, your mind, and your spirit. The thing is so definite, as well as exquisite, that you instinctively search for its sources and reasons, knowing that, in them, there is the still fuller joy of comprehension.

Overhead, far as eye will go, spreads a sky which is brilliantly lit by the sun and yet has a blue, wispy softness. It suggests a bridal veil, hung down for humanity by the angels of Heaven, but always kept among the stars, as it is such a shining raiment. So its freshness remains untarnished, angels being immortal in dress as in being, and the bridal veil is really their signal, fluttered and flown to the sparkling Jhelum in the Vale of Kashmir.

Nearer are the towers and turrets of the Himalayas, arrogant, yet resigned, gaunt yet coloured, a wall where an Indian sun chases white winter, and, in turn, is chased by it. Perhaps, on one of those stately, stubborn mountains you will see a rift which the eye conceives as a Jacob's Ladder of invitation to ascend and explore Heaven itself. Or there is no rift beckoning aloft, no lantern saying, "Come hither"; only blank, immutable, prehistoric rock scraping the welkin in awesome silence. Either sight makes a page in the picture-book of one's memory.

Beside you, fed from the high and the half-way mountains, is a landscape clad in the lush softness of natural fertility and the graciousness of a natural garden. Elemental struggles have been fought out between the gods in the heavens and the devils in the Himalayas, and the surviving essence of Nature has gently fallen on the banks of the Jhelum. Its head-waters froth from the snows, tearing with them, from the grey rocky soil, what they can seize and carry. But its other waters come from a thousand gracious springs, in the bowels of the Asiatic earth, and from kindly burns and rivulets which, like Tennyson's "Brook," "chitter, chatter, as they flow to join the brimming river," all making a gentle countryside.

So the Jhelum is born from Olympian heights and influences, and cradled in a valley of velvet, and, maybe, that explains its majestic dignity and its soft graciousness, because its secret of personality is a blend of both. Away there lies the Gilgit Road, hard and dangerous, no joy-road, except to high venturers who have trodden it all down history; a road of suffering and tragedy, of defeat and conquest, the key to the real Hindu Kush; a stony road in all senses. Down here, where the Jhelum flows, soft beauty is the mantle, as if a Kashmir shawl of magic size and colour were wound round the feet of a giant precipice to keep them warm. "Kashmir . . . without an equal! Kashmir . . . equal to Paradise," is a song the pilgrims of time have sung to the lazy, potent swing of the Jhelum around Srinagar.

Asiatic Venice! City of the Sun! The hoopoes, birds mentioned in Aristophanes under another name, chirp that to the floating city, from beneath their impertinent crests, and the bulbuls take up the praise. You hear its cadence in the long cry of the boatmen of the river as they pole their *doongas* along, or in the quick swish of their *shikara* paddles. The *doonga*, flat-bottomed and enclosed by a wooden framework covered with matting, is the boat of native Kashmir. On it families live, move, and have their being, for it may be at once their home and their means of trading.

Up and down the Jhelum go the *doongas*, which may, in construction, also pass into big cargo-carrying barges. A Kashmiri drops his pole at the nose of his craft and runs backward, along its bulwarks, pushing it up-stream. If it is going down-stream, he is at the stern, holding an even course with the same pole, helped by a rude rudder in the hands of some member of his family, probably the oldest woman, because this is not hard work. A wife or a daughter will be cooking food on a simple stove, which, you fear, may set the ship afire, but rarely does, and dark eyes and covert smiles come across the water. A few children will be about on the living part of a *doonga*, and you may get a whiff of a cow, a calf, a sheep, or even a pig, because what you have is the ark of the Jhelum River.

Do you want to hire a *doonga* and go philandering with the many and various charms of the Jhelum? That was an old fashion of travel in Kashmir, as a relief from too much *tonga*-driving, but now there are possible roads and lots of motor-cars. Even so, why not be a Bohemian and go as you please with a *doonga*, in which you can fit up a bed, store your baggage, and have the boatman, his women, and his progeny, to wait on your pleasure? Not very elegant, perhaps, this life, but easy and uncostly, and, withal, perhaps, romantic, if you wish it to be.

Probably the fine white-man's houseboats, which line the Jhelum along its two shores at Srinagar, have sprung from the use, in the same way, of *doongas* by aforetime European visitors to the Jhelum. Now they have house-boats, with all the amenities of a Thames house-boat and all the comforts of space and service which belong to India. More, if, for any reason, you want to go elsewhere on the bosom of the Jhelum, you simply up-anchor, though there are proper regulations and ordinances about this which must be observed in Sir Hari Singh's domain.

If the Jhelum, coming by many roads, be elusive, then so are the craft that float on it; the houseboat or the *doonga*, the mere carrying barge, or the swift little *shikara*. It is the gondola of this Eastern Venice, with graceful lines, sofa-like seats, for two or more, and paddlers behind curtains, drawn or not drawn. "*Shikara, shikara, shikara!*" So the boatmen shout their wares, and your payment, with a tip added, is very modest, set beside the sweet company you may have, the quiet glide through the water, the soothing stroke of the paddles, now fast, now slow, and the feeling of quiet contentment which captures you in the embrace of the Jhelum.

Its *ghats*, or "places," along the banks are a particular sight, in colour and movement, when the Maharaja of Kashmir has a river procession. His boats are gay in aspect and manned with gaily-clad rowers, and they swing along at a fine speed. Native Srinagar turns out and cries shrill greetings, or just looks on, for the Kashmiri is really not a demonstrative person. He might subscribe to the saying, "He also serves who only stands and waits," but he likes to see his lovely river braided with high colour and high spirits.

Down-stream go the jolly boats, and not only are the banks alive with onlookers, but also the endless houses and shops which line them. Mats are hung from windows, and men and women, in the loose garments of the East, lean out, agog and yet reticent. Many of those men are shopkeepers, looking from their shop windows, and they will beckon you to come and buy their wares. That can be an amusing and rather exhausting effort, because it means bargaining, and success in it needs accomplishments which you may or may not possess. But you'll enjoy the experience and its subtle ways, including, perhaps, the invitation: "Come to-morrow again and take a cup of real Thibet tea. You need not buy, just come!"

Don't let that, or anything else, come between you and the picturesqueness of Srinagar, as you beat along its miles of water front, the High Street of the Jhelum. Old, old temples, worn stairs which led to them, open-ended houses, roofs covered with grass in which irises and poppies flame, a mixture of mediæval Europe and of India! That is the show you pass, with the original Maharajal Palace standing out importantly into the Jhelum. Also successive bridges leaning towards you in queer arches, as if they wished to whisper what sighs and laughter they have heard from those crossing them since they were built, some of them ages ago.

Stout fellows are the boat-men of the Jhelum, though not, maybe, stouter-hearted than other Kashmiris. They wear the same strangely effeminate gown, but the activities of their calling sometimes demand freedom from it, and then you see how lithe a Jhelum body can be. More often than not, those boatmen cannot swim, and though accidents are not common, the ancient Hydaspes has currents and depths where life and death might meet in an instant. You feel, indeed, that it has some of the mystery of the other world, as well as the beauty of this, and that leaves you marvelling on still another thing in Kashmir.

XVI. BESIDE THE SHALIMAR!

Pale hands I loved beside the Shalimar,
Where are you now? Who lies beneath your spell!
Whom do you lead on Rapture's roadway, far,
Before you agonise them in farewell?

* * * * *

Pale hands, pink-tipped, like Lotus buds that float
On those cool waters where we used to dwell,
I would have rather felt you round my throat
Crushing out life, than waving me farewell.

"Kashmiri Love Song," by Laurence Hope.

PERHAPS the modern reader is most familiar with the Shalimar Garden of Kashmir in the note of passion which the gifted Anglo-Indian lady who was "Laurence Hope" wound about it. She was thinking of it in the Mogul days, as we also shall do when we enter its gates, wander on its velvet grass, and enjoy the sparkle of its waters, for here the past is married to the present.

Royal gardens! That is what the name means, as its neighbour in beauty, the Nishat Bagh, is the Zephyr Garden, or, more poetically, the Garden of the Morning Wind. You may see red-cheeked

WHERE TIME

Past and present in a corner of the Dal Lake;
a Mogul-built bridge, a Kashmiri dwelling, a

English children playing in one, or the other, or both gardens, merry little folk, gathering the wild gowans, as they might in Devonshire, for Kashmir, you have long ago learned, is a white man's land in climate. So, at the Shalimar, you encounter a two-fold atmosphere, tragic emotions and high doings come down on the wings of history, and the gentle peace and graciousness of to-day.

You have, looking far back across the clouds of time, the Shalimar of the Moguls, a place vibrant with—

Splendours and glooms and glimmering incarnations
Of hopes and fears and twilight fantasies ;

the " forest murmurs " of Wagner's " Valkyries." But that Shalimar was also the " Siegfried " of summer skies and scented winds, an ever-vernal epic in landscape. It so remains, for its spell enters your soul, your mind, your body, and from somewhere, Nature's salute to a Paradise, comes :

Such a soft, floating witchery of sound
As twilight Elfins make, when they at eve
Voyage on gentle gales from Fairy-land.

How Coleridge, with his exquisite spirit for the poetry of a countryside, would have loved to sit in the Shalimar and muse ! You can be alone there at some hours, sole possessor of a garden old in tradition, and modern in its beauty, for true beauty is eternal.

Perhaps Jehangir's favourite of the harem, Nur Mahal an earlier, fainter Mumtaz of Shah Jahan's Taj Mahal, was sitting where you are when she said, "This fountain has come from the springs of Paradise." Woman-like, she instinctively felt that a real secret of Kashmir's charm is its many waters, while a man of the Moguls—men, royal or not, being less delicately instinctive—might have got no further than a generality. The springs of Achebal, Bawan, and Vernag are no longer bypaths of pleasure for Akbars, Jehangirs, and Shah Jahans, but their outflow is as full and sweet as ever, and when you count them in hundreds you understand the emerald-green carpet of the Shalimar.

Big, leafy chenar trees, nodding with the grave dignity of centenarians, for they live to a long age; the spiritual deodar, whispering to the breeze that it is the tree of the divinities; the Kashmir fir, brother in appearance to the Scots fir, holding itself stoutly, in contrast to the swaying poplar; the shivering birch, like an elegant woman's body in evening dress; the nervous willow bending and pulling as if it were a young race-horse; and here and there the cherry tree and the apple tree in radiant bloom! Their embranched flowers curtsy to those rising out of the earth, where their roots have been kept warm all the winter by a mantle of snow and given new fructification by the spring sun. Tulips lift themselves above a riot of lesser blooms, all making the earth glorious, and the iris is, in itself, a constant Kashmir splendour.

Ask, if you understand flower language, why it is so plentiful, and it will tell you an unexpected story. There is something in the appearance, or smell, of the iris which cattle do not like, even the ever-curious, if privileged Indian cow, and they avoid it. Its roots, strong and thick, gather an area of soil together so firmly that it is not easily distributed. The Kashmiris bury their dead in graves which are rude and not, as a rule, very deep. Therefore, to keep the cattle away and to discourage wandering jackals from being resurrectionists, they plant their holy grounds with irises of whatever colour may happen.

Apparently this has always been done, and the Kashmiri iris has become far-flung, for the other reason that it seeds itself. The winds carry it where they list, from a lonely grave to a cultivated field, from that field to a valley or hill, and thus the splendour grows. Its velvety bloom greets you everywhere, like a banner, and could its birthright as a particular Kashmir flower rest on more tender associations? Other flowers are more intimate, but watch the iris carpeting the Shalimar, or the Chenar Bagh, meaning the

Garden of Plane Trees, aforetime sacred to bachelors, now not so sacred, and you will understand once more why the Moguls so loved Kashmir.

Its tender flowers hug the valleys, as its hardy goats strike for the high places, because they cannot eat the grass of the *nullahs*. "In the time of flowers," say the Kashmiris, as they say, "In the time of the Mulberries you will catch many fish at Simbal," or "When the maze is ripe the bears come from the jungle." Everywhere, in this earth of ours, Mother Nature lives upon herself, sometimes a cannibal, but always beautiful. John Keats might have been in the Shalimar Garden, the air "cooling and so very still," when he wrote of English flowers that "Had not yet lost those starry diadems, caught from the early sobbing of the morn."

He might, in his subtle poet's fancy, even have heard beautiful Nur Mahal sobbing, in lovely loneliness, because she and Jehangir had quarrelled. We, ourselves, were directly instructed about the quarrel, made enduringly familiar to the West in Thomas Moore's "Lalla Rookh," by a Kashmiri gentleman who took us round the Shalimar. Standing beside the shining, black, marble pillars of its pavilioned fountain, he supposed Nur Mahal to be near and saying, in language which, perhaps, he found for her:

Oh, thou waterfall! For whose sake have you been moaning?
For whose grief have you got wrinkles on your forehead?
Is it because, like myself, you have been striking your head against these stones
On account of some great grief?

Our Kashmiri gentleman with the romantic soul was not content merely to give us the dirge he supposed Nur Mahal to have crooned to herself! He had it that Jehangir heard her, and, knowing the way of women in love and distress, went instantly and took her in his arms, so happily ending a lovers' quarrel, which Thomas Moore, in his "Lalla Rookh," brings to a close with the familiar lines:

And well do vanished frowns enhance
The charms of every brightened glance;
And dearer seems each dawning smile
For having lost its light a while;
And happier now, for all her sighs,
As on his arms her head reposes,
She whispers him with laughing eyes,
"Remember, love, the feast of roses."

He must have been a good lover, this most chivalrous Mogul, Jehangir, and, indeed, there are many tributes to it. Tragedy fell into his life, as it mostly has fallen into the lives of great lovers, the joy, and then the sorrow ordained for them. There is more direct evidence of his colourful and sentimental spirit in a passage he wrote while he was somewhere on the Indian war-path.

"I marched," it reads, "the whole way through the bed of a river, in which water was then flowing and the oleander bushes were in full bloom and of exquisite colour like peach blossoms. I ordered my personal attendants, both horse and foot," it goes on, "to bind branches of the flowers in their turbans, and I directed that the turbans of those who would not decorate themselves in this fashion should be taken off their heads. I thus got up a fine garden"; and surely, one may add, it was an unusual one.

Shalimar survives, well kept by the reigning Maharaja of Kashmir, to testify how fondly the Moguls regarded their pleasure-gardens. They could let their subjects salute them in such artificial and sounding language as "To the seat of excellence and exalted worth, the abode of learning and accomplishments," or "To the abode of bravery and enterprise, the high and exalted in rank." But, with their gardens, they were human, feeling, "God wot," that in them there was the spirit of a Providence higher than any Mogul.

Before you, looking down from the green incline of the Shalimar, stretches the Dal Lake, and half its surface is a-bloom with the lotus, in colours as dainty as my lady's cheeks in Bond Street, and more natural. Floating flowers, and floating islands, too, for the Kashmir lake-men compose these from reeds which they cut, deep down in the water. Freed, they rise to the surface, become matted together, and then earth is spread on them, and in this earth seeds are sown. So the floating islands become small floating gardens, where the melon and the cucumber or some other vegetable flourishes, utility the handmaid of beauty.

Such silver-clear water as that of the Dal Lake there cannot be anywhere else in the world. Look into it, and you start as if something had unveiled you. It catches even shadows in such deep detail, though softly, exquisitely, that it makes them seem realities. It might be a mirror for fairies or a bath for naiads, and it is cool with the breath of the sun-crested Himalayas. One might liken it to iced champagne in a huge bowl, formed by a dent in the Himalayas.

What carousings the Moguls had on the Dal Lake, attuned to all the moods of sex and sentiment, and, maybe, you toy with the thought that you would like to be a modern Mogul. What *shikara* or house-boat wonders you can seek on the Dal to-day—yea, or this very night—for there is nothing here to frighten romance. Seek it at a witching hour when the Indian moon is all in love, and you will surely gather a memory which may become a poem. For the Dal Lake is "Paradise enow," to be serenaded as George Darley serenaded a lovely woman:

Sweet in her green, all the flower
of beauty slumbers,
Lulled by the faint breezes
sighing through her hair.

A SWEET WATER OF ASIA

An idyllic way from the Dal Lake to the Nishat Bagh, one of the Mogul pleasure-gardens.

XVII. EVE IN A KASHMIR EDEN

If woman can make the worst wilderness dear,
Think, think what a Heav'n she must make of
Cashmere.

" Lalla Rookh."

" *Your eyes are like Narcissuses, and when I look at them, I feel as if I were under the influence of wine.*"

Kashmiri Dancing Song.

THE beauty of the women of Kashmir has been a song of the ages in the Orient, and its melody came to the Occident and lingered. Eastern beauty; but this token of the Gods is as magic in a dark skin, draped in black hair, as in a white skin draped in fair hair. It has no boundaries, no bonds, and it conquers a universal salute, because always the secret of it is the lamp of soul, of mind and of body which is within, and the portal thereto lies in the eyes.

The eyes of a beautiful Kashmiri woman have such an urgency, mingled with pathos, that you look into them as you would look into spring waters, wondering. She may be old, in which case they have the glaze of life, braided with the hope of something more, and better, to come. Is she middle-aged? They have a softer shade of memory and a clearer gleam of romance still awaited. Is she a young wife, or a girl? and the way between the two is no more than a rose-walk. Then her eyes are large, inquiring, dark as the eyelashes falling over them, shining, like an April morning in Kashmir, with a bewitching double-light of emotion and instinct.

Kashmiri eyes like the stars! No; eyes which are their own stars, because they gather into them both the physical beauty and the spiritual clouds of the Kashmiri woman, who is a primal creature of her Garden of Eden. They are, in general, almond-shaped, and so have room for laughter or tears, and always they have a touch of the just dumb animal, a lamb or a calf, an ox or a horse. They glow like great lanterns placed to light her figure, which may be poorly robed, with single colours of red and blue or, perhaps, yellow, or merely plain cotton. But there will certainly be grace of body, thanks to the elastic walk which her barefootedness gives her.

Similarly, her action with her hands or her head will be graceful, as when she swings a scull or wields a pole in a Jhelum *doonga*, or carries a jar of water on her head from the nearest spring. Her trinkets clatter on her ankles, swing heavily from her ears, braid her hair, or hang, a wealth of hazardous stones, round her neck. But ever you return to the liquid languor of her eyes, to the physical joy and coquetry which shine in them, to their softness, as if they were a mixture of the Kashmir iris, the Kashmir tulip, and the Kashmir pansy—all flowers with a Himalayan coolness and the warmth of the Indian sun.

If those eyes do not say " Come hither," it is only because they do not need to say it, and, moreover, that would be a boldness in the delicate femininity of India. They are eyes which look at you unashamed, and therefore you may look at them unabashed, but, maybe, their rainbow of womanliness guards a whole temple of love and passion, because Kashmir is Kashmir, where romance is inborn and June is flaming.

Give the Kashmiri woman her fine white teeth, " quarelets of pearls," which sometimes she colours, and you confirm the spell of her eyes. For, East or West, flashing eyes and gleaming teeth are weapons which keep a love-lorn lad on tenterhooks. " Here," you say to yourself, " are the Parisians of the East, only they have an English rosiness of complexion behind the Eastern tan and a natural graciousness which might be Italian." All this means a certain physical originality which both wins you and makes you curious.

Often you encounter faces no darker than those of the sun-burned women of Naples, and often, also, you are struck with the almost whiteness of a Kashmiri woman and with the almost Greek contour of her face. Reflect, again, that Alexander the Great passed through Northern India, leaving many of his soldiers to settle there, as the wrecked Spaniards of the Elizabethan Armada settled in Cornwall and on the West Coast of Ireland, also leaving their human imprint. There had, too, been a link of race between the Kashmiris and the Persians, so that fairly white skins in a natively brown land are not astonishing. You will be told in Kashmir that Jehangir's beloved Nur Mahal of the Shalimar, was herself a typical Kashmiri, and when a beautiful woman is concerned there are no doubts at the time, and there must be no questionings afterwards.

The boat-women of the Jhelum river, like their men, are known for their handsome appearance and their picturesque air. Observe, when you have recovered from the spell of their almond eyes and the thrill of their lithe, easy movements, for in both ways they notably command a wayfarer. Notice their laughing faces, their flowing head-dresses, and the tremor in those loose gowns of theirs, with the large sleeves. They probably wear a fillet of red cloth on the forehead, topped by a sort of white mantilla. Their hair is done in long plaits, which are then gathered together and finished with a tassel. They are bigger in frame than the average Indian woman, and that applies to Kashmir generally; "d——d fine women," a Western buck of the old days would have said, and if he knew India and Indian poetry he might have quoted:

Brunettes and the Banyan's shadow
Well-springs and a brick built wall
Are all alike cool in the summer,
And warm in the winter—all!

Tradition associated the river folk of the Jhelum with a particular Indian tribe of Gypsy blood which supplied the prettiest Nautch girls in India to " troll the tongue and roll the eye." An open-air life for long years must also have had its health-giving, handsome-giving results, and there is another thing. The Jhelum boat-folk, being a folk peculiar to themselves, have not been bound either by the Moslem or the Hindu canons, but have lived and loved as they cared or could. Pagan Mother Nature seems to have prospered this, just as English love children are often most beautiful, and sometimes most gifted mentally.

Nature's brood have Nature's ways, and all women in Kashmir know that the length of an eyelash and a touch of antimony add to the beauty of a hazel eye. They " do " their faces in their Eastern fashion, but always the soft, fine pinkness under the skin looks out like a blushing, captivating rose at dawn. The folk-lore of the country tells us that young girls have to keep an eye half open while they sleep, lest the fairies, jealous of their beauty, should come and steal the antimony from their eyes. They could not steal the marks of caste which will, perhaps, be on the brow of a Kashmir Hindu lady, an Indian echo of what Moses ingeminates in the Book of Deuteronomy:

Therefore shall ye lay up these, my words, in your heart, and in your soul, and bind them for a sign upon your hand, that they may be as frontlets between your eyes.

Of the ladies of Kashmir the stranger sees nothing, because they live in *purda*, with little outward light or human touch. Probably they have their own ideas about the open world, and a natural and growing desire to be let into it. But they would hardly understand how a woman could become a great hunter, even if they met her in their own land, for there she was; a real, mighty hunter, mind you, who had shot her tiger, year after year, in the jungles of India.

She had, her story was, gone from England to India, and been filled with its sense of adventure, and soon she found herself a *shikarri*. She learned to take the roughness of the jungle as it came, asking no quarter because she was a woman, and it had all been splendid. Perhaps her most exciting adventure was with a bear which she followed into a cave, where he gave fight with his back to the wall. A favourite trick with the Indian bear is to pull the scalp from a man or woman, but, happily, it did not get to that with this Diana of England, so completely in contrast to the women of Kashmir, ladies or commonalty.

Love-philtres and perfumes are the inheritance of the Kashmiri woman, when she is not born so lowly that she must toil the fields with, or for, her man, the destiny which mostly awaits her. Child-marriage is now wholly forbidden in the State, by decree of the Maharaja, and therefore the girl-mother, a sad figure, to our eyes, however gaily she may be dressed, is passing out. She dates far back in the history of India, and one reason for her institution was the care the universal mother has for the child of her body. When the rude mountaineers of India were, long ago, in the habit of raiding the Plains, they took the young girls, among other booty. There arose the custom of marrying, or betrothing those young girls, as a protection, because then they would no longer seem desirable to the northern tribesmen, and that is one origin of child-marriage, though, to be sure, there are others.

It might be an interesting speculation, if it could be made, whether the long-fabled beauty of Kashmir women was known to Solomon, in all his glory, with all his wives. And did he throw his matrimonial net as far as the Jhelum

River, for there is the authority of an English drinking song that he made a wide sweep:

King Solomon took ten thousand wives,
From Tarshish and from Tyre,
With a concubine from Samarkand
Whenever he might require.
But whether he fetched 'em fat or lean,
Or whether tall or short,
There were no flies on the shy gazelles
King Solomon took to court.

XVIII. THE GOWNED KASHMIRI

Listen to the Salutation of the Dawn :
Look to this day,
For it is life, the very life of life,
In its brief course lie all the
Varieties and realities of existence :
The bliss of growth
The glory of action,
The splendour of beauty ;
For Yesterday is but a dream
And To-morrow is only a vision,
But To-day well-lived makes
Every Yesterday a dream of happiness,
And every To-morrow a vision of hope.
Look well, therefore, to this day !
Such is the salutation of the Dawn.

From the Sanskrit.

NOWHERE could the natural elements which make and mould human life be more inspiring, more kindly, more helpful in a hundred ways, than in the Happy Valley of Kashmir. What sort of men have they thrown up, and do they hear the Salutation of the Dawn as a Sermon on their Himalayan Mount ?

Perhaps not, because they have not yet come

to any fuller philosophy of existence than is contained in their religions, Moslem or Hindu, and in their deadening daily toil. They are primitive, untutored as we should say, just a raw, simple people of the soil. But Kashmiri men have been a long, long time, and they have their inheritance of customs, characteristics, and personality.

Akbar, the story goes, thought so little of them, in his martial Mogul day, that he disrobed them of all Oriental caparisoning and ordered them to wear woollen cloaks, hanging to their ankles. "Men!" said he; "faint-hearts, not lion-hearts, therefore skirts for you." His order is their dress to-day, habit, once it is enforced or adopted, being part of us all. But nightgown-like cloaks notwithstanding, they are often fine fellows to the eye, though not a match in handsomeness for their women, whose dark eyes and red lips outshine the Jhelum. If Kashmir has no martial history except invasions, how could Akbar expect its people to be natural-born warriors? They threw up no great leaders of their own to mould a stern national character, and so we have a country and a race never valorous, but ever colourful. It is a still picture of delicate, finely-woven threads, not one of high drama, like the prancing story of the Sikhs or the Rajputs.

Peace, we know, has its victories as well as war, and one of them in Asia, for what it is worth, is the Kashmiri man, deep black of hair, dark brown of skin, languishing of eye, white-toothed and smiling, most likely shapely of body and limb, a native you like on sight, partly because, as you perceive, he is willing to like you. He is gay, elastic both of body and mind, there differing from the Indian below the Himalayas, who never sits on a fence and looks at the sun and laughs with sheer physical joy.

The Kashmiri may be the humblest creature, in station and possessions, a desert in flesh, for want of nourishing food, shivering in the cold weather, because he is ill-clad. Even when he squats on his brazier of charcoal, with the folds of his gown gathered about it and his legs, he is still cold. But he has a relish of life, begotten atmospherically of the Happy Valley, which nurtures him spiritually, though he may not show great signs of it, and gives him his contented, hopeful temperament and accepting outlook.

Perhaps the Kashmiri's comparative singleness of race has made it easier for him to keep his type. Passing the centuries in this recess of India, he is less composite, less mongrel, than most of her peoples. He has been free from the stimulation of violence, because he has let more vigorous races come in succession and go in succession, and the corroding lust of ill-gotten gain has not been his. His schooling has been to take what came, a sort of Kismet—not the teaching of a blow for a blow, and let yours be got in first. There has resulted an expression of olive-oil softness, home-grown in the sunniest spots, a Kashmiri good-nature, a character suited for the crafts of life more than for its strenuous occasions.

There is hardly anything, you discover, that a Kashmiri craftsman will not do well, once he gets down to it. Take the making of paper-maché, which is a famed speciality of Srinagar, or silver-working, still an older trade on the banks of the Jhelum. Wood carving, too, which finds ingenious and artistic forms, mostly in walnut, still a precious wood in the northern forests of India, though our " bright young people " might call furniture made of it " Victorian."

Clever boat-building is natural in a land of many waters, and in a land of flowers gardening is almost ordained in the coolie who comes to the Sahib's garden. The skins of wild animals trapped in the Himalayas give the Kashmiri another trade in which he is expert, for he cures them well. The furriers of London or Paris or New York are left to do the rest, though a visiting Memsahib to Srinagar will easily find what she needs all ready for the tempestuous Himalayas, or even for the elegance of a dinner-party in the cold weather of India. And she can have a lovely time bargaining with the fur-merchants of Srinagar, who are full of Eastern courtesy and persuasion, never in a hurry, and manageable, if deftly handled.

The Kashmiri man, merchant, boatman, or *ryot*, looks his feelings more than speaks them, in this resembling his women, though always less eloquently. You fancy that you detect a streak of sentiment in him, if only because that is a quality native to mountain peoples everywhere. But, in his case, it has more relationship to gentleness than to chivalry, and it may be illustrated, as it was to me, by supposing that a Kashmiri servant is dismissed by his Sahib master, after many warnings.

" Serve him right," all the other native servants will say, and they may make a chorus of forty or fifty voices ; " he is no good, and we have seen it." By and by they will come to the Sahib, saying, " He can find nothing to do and starves—he and his wife and children. Please will you not take him back, Sahib, and we will see he isn't lazy and useless any more ? " The heart of the Kashmiri may be soft, but one could scarcely, so far as he is concerned, draw the lesson that it " makes us right or wrong," as Robert Burns sang. Certainly it is impossible for a Western onlooker in the East to say more than, " Things seem so, but this is the Orient, an old world new to us." He will realise that it has as many folds as a thousand Kashmir shawls, and then continue his pilgrim's way.

"Do not admit a Kashmiri to your friendship," an Indian wisdom-while-you-wait has it, "or you will hang a hatchet over your door." Even crueller is the saying, "Many fowls in a house will defile it, and many Kashmiris in a country will spoil it." A one-time traveller among them dwelt on the curious contrast between the often Herculean build of a peasant and his "whining complaints and timid disposition." Catch that giant telling lies, as might, perhaps, be done, for a lie is a compromise, a subtlety, an evasion most likely in an unheroic national character, and his excuses were "so ready, so profuse, and so comical" that our traveller merely smiled. There, and in such views, we have the civilian version of Akbar's, "You Kashmiris have only stomachs to eat, not to fight," and he ordered them to eat their victuals cold.

Well, the case of the Kashmiri *ryot* is *sukkut*, meaning hard and difficult, and his *puttoo*, or homespun, covers many cares. So the gentleness of the valley, after ingeminating itself into its men, as, with more welcome effects, into its women, becomes, possibly, a subtlety, a craftiness capable of being also "slimness." You cannot have, in a race, a personality which is both strong and flabby, but must be content with what is good in it, and make the best of what is less good.

Wherever you turn in Kashmir this breath of

softness meets you in various forms; a universality of satin-texture in the Himalayan setting of stark grandeur. Indeed, is it not world-wide news that its water softens a shawl better than any other water whatsoever? and you should see the Kashmiri women washing their shawls in the silvery Dal Lake. They are primitively innocent of small sins, for they will not know, being no smokers, that tobacco grown in Kashmir has not the pungency of that grown elsewhere. Generally, you have only to feel the peculiar softness of the atmosphere to grasp all this and many other things, which cannot be communicated in words, for they are only sensations.

The Kashmiri man, in appearance only, is often likened to the militant Afghan and the stalwart Afridi. The three races have large, aquiline features, and skins which have well been described as "subdued Jewish." There the resemblance ends, as came home very clearly to us one fine April morning when there was a parade of sleek, frisky polo-ponies in a Jhelum side garden. The head groom was an Afridi, fair of hair and almost of skin, big-boned and athletic. One of the ponies kicked about in such an unsilken, violent way, that the gathered Kashmiri servants scurried away, timid and alarmed, though two score in number. The Afridi man, who rode the beast, never shook in his saddle, and by great horsemanship soon had it quiet and obedient, and then the Kashmiris returned, vastly relieved. They were bred in a valley of concord, where life, meagre as it might be, has always been easy; while he came from marches where the climate is more severe, where it is a struggle to live, and where, consequently, stronger men grow.

But in the higher, outer parts of Sir Hari Singh's "delectable duchy" there are men who, having a constant struggle with Nature, are stern, as well as strong. They are typified by the Gujars, who lived wildly by plunder in Mogul times, and now are tamed to be herdsmen. Their queer houses, made of beaten earth, have flat roofs, and you can hardly see them against a hillside. But their clothes attract, dull reds and smoky blues being true colours for paths leading through the greenery of grass and trees, starred by flowing waters.

You are instructed that the Kashmiris rarely fight among themselves, being unquarrelsome by virtue of their ease of character. That, and their poverty, make for the larger peace of the community, and word battles are, generally, the worst disturbances you will meet among the boat-folk of the pillowy Jhelum, or among the jostling populace in the narrow, wandering streets of Srinagar. Would a new and stronger manhood have developed among the Kashmiris if we had kept their country in our own hands, and the British Tommy, garrisoning India, in it through-

THE CITY OF Srinagar, the Kashmiri capital, with the deep, swinging Jhelum as its great artery of traffic

out the Indian summer? Students of human nature might have been interested to watch the consequences of such a contact between energy and "Kismet." But the Kashmiri himself would, most likely, just have smiled his subtle, dreamy, lotus-like smile and remained indifferent, because sufficient unto himself is the day and to-morrow may never come, who knows?

XIX. A MAHARAJA AT HOME

You are in your own Kingdom.
Virgil.

Heavens! what a goodly Prospect spreads around.
James Thomson.

YOU can hardly know Kashmir unless you meet its Maharaja, for he is its chief and overlord, its prince and its king, its all in all in government, within the Indian sceptre of the British Raj. So it was good to get a large, generous, really inviting card inscribed: " The Maharaja of Jammu and Kashmir at home at the Gulab Bhawan Palace . . ."

" A horse! a horse! my kingdom for a horse," cries a King in Shakespeare, but there was no need to ride palace-ward in that haste. There was full time to reflect, with Bacon, that " Princes "—Indian or otherwise—" are like to heavenly bodies which cause good or evil times, and which have much veneration, but no rest." We are to make a modern instance of the old Baconian wisdom by invading the Gulab Bhawan Palace of Sir Hari Singh.

He is the inheritor of traditions which hold

the history and the colour of India, but he himself is simplicity. You see that when you meet him, you feel it when you talk with him, and he speaks English so well that a slight accent is only noticeable for its melody. And he talks to us of London, saying, " It is a much better place than Paris. Not so pretty, but kindly and understandable, all the more because I know English and not French."

" One can get on quite well in France without knowing French," it was suggested to him.

" Oh, no," he answered; " to be at home in a foreign country you must know its language."

" Possibly," it was also suggested, " the great human quality of London is its motherliness."

He nodded an understanding nod, and said that some day he would like to visit America, but, he added, " I would fear to go unless I had somebody to chaperone me." He was thinking of the hugeness and variety of America, and of the known hospitality of its people.

Travel he likes, and to see the world, but naturally his heart is in his own land, and perhaps more in his little kingdom of Jammu, though it is plain, than in Kashmir, which is unchallengeably beautiful. Old Jammu of his old family; the newer Kashmir come to it; and that explains these things. Jammu reassures him, because it is Singh, and, for all the rest of the world cares, will remain Singh. Kashmir is a land into which the stranger and his ways have penetrated, because it is an Indian garden of Eden. Moreover, the stranger and his ways will probably become still more courting, as Kashmir has great natural potentialities.

Even so, Sir Hari Singh is one of the most broad-minded and enlightened of the Indian ruling princes. His very definite personality is gloved in a friendly charm; a ruler of breeding and kindliness, letting his robes of state fall away from him for a time. He is a clean-cut, highly educated, admirably informed man, and all that shines out of his black, closely set eyes. The face is regular and mobile in expression, the forehead broad, the nose aquiline, the mouth sensitive, the chin graceful and firm. It is a face you would notice in a crowd, and the figure, dressed in dark brown, with tight-fitting Jodhpore breeches and brown shoes, has an equal air of distinction.

The Maharaja is tall, one was going to say for an Indian, but that would be stupid, because the races which inhabit the heights of India have stature, as well as physical grit. He moves quickly, animatedly, always observantly, holding his own in any conversation, whether it be about the snowy, winter climate of Kashmir, which he does not like, or with a clever, beautiful English-woman, whose presence he naturally does appreciate, like the rest of us.

Oh, yes, our English folk, gathered for tea at

his new palace in Kashmir, includes a lady who is both sunshine and moonbeam, and a British Raj, who has won administrative fame in India and a name for his witty talk. Gallant Maharaja, Gallant proconsul! Her little ladyship, hatted, gowned, silk-stockinged like an English blush-rose, and silver-shoed like the snow on the Himalayas, is heroine to both. She manages them very well, holding them in austere balance, so that it is an hour's social tournament, in which the Prince of India and the Pro-Consul of England are equal victors for wit, wisdom and chivalry; and they have the still greater satisfaction of knowing that her ladyship has conquered both.

A sense of gay humour is a vast endowment to find in one's cradle, and the Maharaja of Kashmir has it in a nimble, subtle form. He can tell a story and polish it with a smile, crack a joke and expound it with a glint of his eye, remain silent and yet speak with his changing expression. A man who is sure of himself, like a woman who knows just how far to go, can always be diverting, even when the company to be diverted is assorted. See the Maharaja of Kashmir, hospitable on his native heath, and you will see also that he is always himself; and indeed he has every reason for being himself.

Whose window in the whole wide world has the view of his, from the Gulab Bhawn Palace? The Dal Lake below, a dreaming water of sun and shadow, of green and gold, of floating gardens and flying birds, of *shikaras* and house-boats. Beyond, the Himalayas range themselves in tiers of green, then brown, then white, and the sun lights them in all their stages skyward. Your eye follows their shoulder-to-shoulder spires on the left, until they are lost on one side ; or you can follow other spires on the right until they also are lost in space. Here might be an army of huge soldiers, like the old White Guards of the Russian Tsar, on sentinel duty over the Maharaja of Kashmir's happy valley, lest anything should disturb it.

His palace is, for the afternoon, a home for English people away from home, all glad to share, not only his company, but the loveliness of this, his kingdom. It is that, don't forget, for he is the master, the superior, the holder of it and its well-being in every sense, human and material. Surely the responsibility is great, but the opportunities are also great, and a tea-party from the Western world may be a stimulus to the grasping of them. You cannot have two civilisations meet in good fellowship without some new sparks being struck in the brotherliness which knits all mankind, rough-hew it as mankind will.

The Maharaja's band of musicians, wearing loose red coats and loose white knickerbockers, play in a corner of his gardens, first the tune which may be called the anthem of his house. Soldiers in colour and khaki mount guard, a small cohort of household servants makes splendour at the doorsteps of the palace, and on the green and pleasant grass rise two large tents with tea-tables, cosy chairs, and many beautiful rugs. Time has no meaning for the clock in the land of the lotus, and jokes go round and merry chat. Exquisite tea, seductive ices, gleaming liqueurs, brandy-and-sodas, cigars, cigarettes, they all circulate in cheerfulness, and, one notices, are accepted with delicate austerity.

That is the personal note which lies behind this passing but picturesque hour, and you associate it with the Maharaja himself. "Have you," he asks a favoured guest, "seen the wonderful show of Kashmir products which is on view in Srinagar? It's open for the rest of to-day, and then it comes to an end." "Ah," says the favoured guest, "so it's time we were going." "Nay, nay," answers the Maharaja quickly; "I did not mean that; I only meant I'd like you to see it"; and he did, being courteous and kindly.

Everything comes to an end, even a princely party in a corner of Kashmir where the Moguls are recalled by their gardens of pleasure; and indeed that very day the Nishat Bagh is gay with the dresses of Kashmiris who, keeping a religious holiday, had, earlier, bathed in a miraculous spring by the side of the Dal Lake. We could see them drifting homeward in the eventide, along the modern road of the Maharaja's making, and on the ancient face of the Dal Lake, a roadway of water traffic.

Any human flutter is infectious, and the Maharaja's guests begin to move; definitely when he, noticing this, and not till then, rises from his golden chair and says, "Good evening," to those immediately about him. Then he waves a salute and a salaam to everybody else and walks into his Gulab Bhwan Palace to rest, while—

The dusky night rides down the
Sky, and ushers in the morn.

IDLE AS A
PAINTED SHIP!

A backwater of the Dal Lake, whose negligent peace and sweet, colourful charm are abounding.

XX. "HERE'S FLOWERS FOR YOU!"

Hot lavender, mints, savory, majoram;
The marigold that goes to bed wi' the sun,
And with him rises, weeping: these are flowers
Of middle summer.

"The Winter's Tale."

WHO does not know, even if Shakespeare had never described it, the sweet beauty of an English garden in the long, warm days and the short, sweet nights of summer-time? It can be a little heaven on this wide earth, a God's acre in a living sense, as a sweet church-yard is God's acre in the other sense. Its beauty enshrines the mind, its gentleness comforts the heart, and its life awakens the body to new strength.

You may take that still romance of England to Kashmir and not forget it, because of the many remindful scenes. Not quite the same scenes, for you are far away in Asia among the Himalayas, in a ruder, bigger setting, but kindred in flowers, and birds, and in that which, wherever we meet it, we call poetry. Some Eastern poet was, no doubt, lost in an Eastern garden when he said to him-self:

The time to quaff delicious wine is now,
For musty scents breathe from the mountain-brow.

So, shall I tell you about a Kashmir garden of which one could not sing too much in the spirit, " I know a bank where the wild thyme grows ? " Everything beautiful to the eye, or good in the nostrils, or both, is easily at home in that garden. Chenar trees, mulberry trees, acacias and wild cherry trees play hide and seek with the dappling rays of the sun. Poplars line up in rows as if to repel invaders, but really to prove that there are many spring waters refreshing this garden, where—

From sky to sod,
The world's unfolded blossoms smell of God.

It is as English a garden as you could fancy, though it lies beneath the Himalayas, where strange things dwell. Birds sing in it, as in England, and there are lots of them, some plain like the Indian thrush or the mina, a kind of pie-bald blackbird, others coloured, like the hoopoe with its speckled plume and saffron neck, the paradise fly-catcher, which is elegant to see and swift on the wing, or the golden oriole, perhaps the most handsome bird you meet in Kashmir. He, with other gay comrades, winters in India and summers in Kashmir, while the plainer birds, such, again, as the jackdaw or the tom-tit, spend the whole year in the mountainous north, despite snows and frosts, though probably many of them die, not, one hopes, the friendly warm-breasted robin.

Birds of the larger order float above our garden on the Jhelum River, which, itself, glides beyond that flowery bund and those very correct poplar trees. A parliament of crows was in session, the other morning on the lawn; either that, we supposed, or as a court summoned to deal with some offender in the realm of crow-land. This it proved, for we made out a black fellow in the middle of the assembly, being attacked and battered by the others, who had condemned him and were now carrying out the sentence.

It was a sentence of death, and the poor devil knew it, and was making frantic attempts to escape. But every time he tried to fly he was knocked down by half a dozen brother crows, ardently bent on the job. They struck him with their claws, stabbed him with their beaks, soon had him unresisting, because half dead, and only left him alone when he lay on his back, a most bedraggled corpse.

He was judged and executed within a few minutes, and we were left wondering what his offence might have been. Theft? Treachery? Cowardice? Or had he merely given offence to the king crow of the crowd, jealous perhaps about a crow lady? Anyhow, he had acquitted his misdemeanour according to the unwritten law, as observant people tell you, of the crow world and, perhaps, of other bird and animal life.

We were sorry for him, and we would have gone to his rescue if there had been time, but presently we had another and larger drama. The noisy to-do had attracted a number of kites, large Indian hawks, rapid and foreboding in flight, which forage on the smaller creatures of the air and earth, and will seize chickens almost from under mothering hens. They were, for this particular reason, in the black book of our host, and he promptly went after his gun and the kites flying overhead. Think of hawk-eyes that enabled them to see a dead crow lying on the grass, from which the living crows had now flown; for it was this morsel of food the kites were after. One would come down, as with a long dive, of course to get a closer view, and another would do the same, and so they manœuvred.

Bang! A kite fell with a dunt into the garden. Bang! Another was down, and the uninstructed person would have supposed that those left flying in the sky would become alarmed and clear off. But the way of the Indian kite, a flesh-lover and not particular about it, is to mark anything dead, or dying, even his own kith and kin, and thus he is also a cannibal. The Kashmir workers in the garden knew as much, and were throwing the dead kites into the air as decoys. One man, a

Sikh who did *shikar* things proudly, even brought out a dead crane which he had got somewhere, and spread it where it could be well seen.

Every now and then a still flying kite, still attracted, came within range of the complete Briton with the gun. For he was a master of it, as of various other weapons of sport, and nearly every shot he fired went between two broad wings up in the sky. After half an hour he had a bag of fourteen kites, all brought down within his own garden, and then he returned to his study and his letters, as if nothing much had happened.

You remember what the French say of the Englishman: "It's a fine morning; let's go out and shoot something." Here was an unplanned Kashmir version of that old raillery, and if a Frenchman falls on it he will probably say: "Those English! They take our jokes and make sport of them. They are marvellous." Certainly marvels are possible in Kashmir, notably in a garden which will always be a fond memory and a rich affection.

Consider the lilies, as King Solomon might have said. A house you could, with luck, come upon in Surrey or Sussex, thought out and planned by the English master, decorated and exquisitely furnished by the English mistress; an enframing, spacious carpet of lawns christened every spring night by the dews of high India, and so kept graciously green; an outer circle of smooth fields and paddocks, holding stables for a dozen champing polo-ponies; a generous kitchen-garden smelling of the earth and fresh vegetables; a scattered canopy of trees shading all the flowers that bloom in Kashmir; a chorus of bird song, and, sweetest of all, Pickie and Mina, Alices in their Wonderland.

Pickie is Patricia, because she was born on Saint Patrick's Day, and Mina is Hermione, only she is not old enough to say all that name yet. Pickie is very wise for her four years, very considerate to mere "grown-ups," a dear small woman of sunny locks and sunny nature. So is Mina, on whom she keeps a mothering eye, for the companionship between them is as tender as their ages.

What deft, dancing little feet Pickie has, and she cannot only pirouette on her toes, but double them in and still pirouette. There was the Russian lady who taught dancing, and said, "But this child is wonderful; where did she get it?" Pickie was not concerned with the question, and went on showing all she could do with her nimble little feet, and laughing for joy.

What a whimsical spirit, teasing and amused, dances in Mina's eyes when she looks sideways through the half-closed lids, and says, without knowing it, "Well?" She leans forward, as if she wanted to reach into your arms; indeed, as if that were really what she did want! What a delicious baby! Then she laughs and runs away, back to Pickie, who, being older, is rightfully in charge of their affairs.

Kashmir has many flowers, but none more radiant, none more lovable than Pickie and Mina hiding from each other, seeking each other, among the irises of Ram Mushi Bagh. Next time you will come with me to the garden they love, and we'll all be as happy as kings, for, indeed, it is a garden of wonderful things—

Where the quiet-coloured end of evening smiles.

XXI. HAIL AND FAREWELL!

Look higher, then—perchance—thou mayst, beyond
A hundred ever-rising mountain lines,
And past the range of Night and Shadow—see
The high-heaven dawn of more than mortal day,
Strike on the Mount of Vision.

Alfred Tennyson.

ONE lingers fondly in the Vale of Kashmir, stimulated mentally, spiritually, and physically, because it is the crown of India, a continent whose dramatic story goes back into the darkness and whose future must ever be a drama to its own many peoples and to us who are the Raj. Before going, may we in this cool, clarifying Himalayan air, turn over a few of our Indian thoughts and impressions; ever so modestly, because they are only passing and personal? Still, we may thus, perhaps, take home to England some picture of the India that has been, some glimpse of the India that is to be.

With us, black is the wear of renouncement, the token of a world well lost, but in India it is golden saffron, a radiant sign, as of the sun. That picturesque fact stages, as in a flash, the chasm of

HAIL TO THE HEIGHTS!

A Himalayan Pass from Kashmir to the Roof of the World, Tibet, China, and No Man's Land.

difference which hangs, like a drop-curtain of God, between the West and the East.

India blazes with light, melts with heat, is filled with golds and purples, violets and translucent greens. Pearls of the Orient might jewel the heavenly dome above it, so delicate and luxurious are the hues. Beneath lies a land clothed with the beautiful or awesome things of creation; great forests, huge rivers, terrible mountains, parched deserts, all teaching the people a worship of colour which is the common note in their various faiths. An atmosphere of warm sun, cool moon, and silvery stars, of wide plain, ranging upland, and tropical foliage, has made them cultured, white-faced Brahmins, red-faced Rajputs, or mere brown-faced peasants and city traders.

Where is Babylonia? Where is Assyria? Their names are but echoes of their dead splendours. Ancient Egypt is only a Pharaoh's mummy, so much dust and bauble rescued from the catacombs of the River Nile. But India, for all her age, possibly as great as theirs, is still vital, aye, and clamorous as to what the future may hold for her and hers.

You feel, thinking quietly in the armchair of Kashmir, that new winds are blowing in this Old World, that what we call "progress" is now a clear thread in the colours of the Indian carpet. But you don't feel that those winds, gusty as they may blow at times, are going to displace the India

Monsoon. India is India, its millions of human beings and their characteristics and habits of life are Indian, and so they will remain.

Always there will be the India that the sun blisters in summer and warms in the winter, that the moon dreams over in soft loveliness, that the stars spangle with their witchery; the India ordained, and its consequenced Adam's breed. But the "moving finger" will write, as it did even in Omar Khayyám's old Persia, and the common prayer is that its writing shall be as a golden book of wisdom.

By common consent the British Raj is the foundation-stone of India as she is now and as, by and large, she must be in years to come. It can be built upon, but if it were overturned, or if we removed it, the whole Indian temple would fall. Thus the passage which lies ahead of the Ship of State is only one of the course, not of walking the plank for anybody, and not, certainly, for scuttling the vessel. The Indian political sea may have its heady waves and its cross-currents, but it is charted, and therefore navigable. Otherwise put, there is the Old India, so deeply sunk in itself that it just goes on, and there is the New India stirring in its womb. Ours is the splendid task of guiding them along together, and, perhaps, we are good pilots in a calm, and even better pilots in a storm.

What we may have to do, as individuals or as

nations, is never more important than how we do it, and that is particularly true of India. One remembers John, Viscount Morley—for he liked to get the double barrel—saying, in his study on Wimbledon Common, that, perhaps, his share in opening the portal of Indian self-government was more satisfying, because actual and assessable, than the best of his works as a man of letters. But imagination must illumine the Indian road, and surely it will, because, as the Marquis Curzon said: "Over the Viceregal Throne there hangs not only a canopy of broidered gold, but a mist of human tears." Perhaps he had in mind, for half that thought, what Tavernier, the French traveller wrote: "The Great Mogul has seven magnificent thrones, one wholly covered with diamonds, the others with rubies, emeralds or pearls."

Our task may be big, because we have to find ways in which East and West shall not only meet in harmony, but govern in agreement. We gave the world the gift of constitutional government, a page of human redemption greater in its benefits than anything the world has known since Christ walked the earth and taught His Christian Socialism. Therefore our new call, in the Great Dependency, should be well within the capacity of the Raj and the Indian. You must never forget that the personal element is behind everything in India, that it reckons in ancestry, names, titles, princes, kings, emperors, for that has been the teaching of its whole chain of history.

"He is a 'Pukka Sahib,'" you hear it said, a complete gentleman, one whose word is his bond even if he need trouble to speak at all. The "Burra Sahib," or Big Sahib, and the "Chota Sahib," or Little Sahib, may be discussable, or even "kucha pukka," which is "half and half," but the "Pukka Sahib" is a king. It is a privilege to fetch him the *chota hazri*, or little breakfast, of the early, fresh Indian morning. More privilege goes with the service to him later of his *hazri*, or full breakfast, his *tiffin*, or lunch, his *chae*, or tea, his *khana*, or dinner and his *chota peg* of whisky-and-soda after the sun has gone down.

The "Pukka Sahib" multiplied, is the Raj, as the Old India will be the New India, with the difference that the Indian nation comes in. That is the natural way of the world, evolution in everything, and our privilege is to help the wheel round, wherever and whenever we can. It may creak sometimes, and we get blamed for the creak or we, ourselves, lay the blame on the eternities. They silently keep their counsel, but if, in India, they were to speak they surely would have a good word for the "Pukka Sahib." That complete English gentleman figures symbolically and typically in a popular Commander-in-Chief of whom one hears that his inspection of a regiment is a most original, a most personal, and therefore a most telling affair.

He does not put it through lots of red-tape drill, but takes the men individually, and talks to them in their own tongues, for a good soldier may also be a good Indian linguist. He slaps the Sikh, a naturally proud fellow, on the shoulder, and asks what news he has from the Sikh country about the crops. He playfully prods the little Ghurka in the stomach, feels whether his belt is tight or not, and says " They are giving you plenty to eat —eh ? " The Sikh and the Ghurka like this, show and proclaim their liking, and a link of brotherly personality is established all through the Indian Army. What is natural and characteristic towards plain, native soldiers, is also natural and characteristic towards high officers. If they go away on leave they get a kindly "Bon Voyage" from that C.I.E., or, if they are fresh arrivals, a message of welcome and the invite, " Let's meet soon."

There we have the sort of " Pukka Sahib " who constitutes the British Raj at his best, a household god of many invocations, from Kashmir to Madras. Even the Indian *ryot*, little as he knows and has, knows the Raj as the overlooking father of the country and relies on him for ultimate deliverance from many troubles. By and by, perhaps, the little brown man of the soil, and his importance, will be more fully understood, and his rise to salvation will be our supreme triumph in India; that and the opening outwards of the doors of Purdah.

When will this revelation come to the women of India? When, indeed? Indian life is betangled, as well as adorned, with caste, religion, tradition, and custom, and the British Raj will, in that regard, just watch and pray. But unless a nation has its women fully in its life, that life is the poorer by half, mentally, and poorer by more than half, in heart.

The roads of all the earth have been long for all the women of the earth, with many hard places to travel. The road of the woman of India has been very long, with very hard places on it. Her survival and her advance, often faint but always pursuing, are the measure of her future. Think that, within memory, Suttee might be the calvary of the Hindu widow, that she said "I ascend my husband's funeral pyre," and did so wearing her gayest attire. Think of the cultured and charming Indian ladies you have met while you have journeyed and draw the contrast.

Even a Hindu mother of sixteen with her daughter of three years old; a child leading a child. The mother a slim, stunted figure in green and gold, worn and sad of face. The little daughter a doll, dressed in red and gold, and like a doll also in expression. The passing India, surely!

A brilliant maharani in the physical bloom of eighteen, and just married, wearing a happy blend of Eastern *sari* and western fashion. Dark of skin, with olive behind the dark; deeply black of eyes, with a velvet softness looking from them ; delicate, sensitive hands set off with one or two Eastern rings ; tapering ankles and shapely feet, silk-stockinged in Paris, slippered in Bombay. The arriving India, surely !

A maharani of age and grey hair, her face distinguished in cast, intellectual in expression and strongly maternal, her knowledge wide, her conversation poetic and delightful. She might be a writer of ballads on the principle that they are the touchstone of a nation and a people. Her sisters of India, high born and not, yield her the homage which fine womanhood will win anywhere. Here is a lady who is the head of a family, a house, or even a state, and so we have an India that can be, because, in cases, it already exists.

Don't think, therefore, that because India has Purdah, her women are without influence, all merely dead souls and neglected bodies. They rule behind the curtains, whether they be seen outside or not ; so guiding the lives of their men as well as shaping those of their children. How, women everywhere being the mothers of men, could it be otherwise ? So, in the fullness of time, the womanhood of India, like India itself, may have a second blooming, free and beautiful as the flight of a flock of pink-winged flamingoes across the Dal Lake of Kashmir.

Scattered thoughts about Old India and awakening India, found on the Road to Kashmir, because it is a far road, with many places of call. Impressions of a traveller in hope, as we should all be, even when we have small rightful knowledge. Reflections nursed in that ancient, lovely cradle of Hindustan, the Vale of Kashmir! And that's all; because the India sun is saying "Good-night" behind the solemn minarets of the Himalayas, and to-morrow it is "Good-bye" to their king's majesty. Sorrowfully, so sorrowfully, yet like all the Sahibs and Memsahibs who have ever been—

I would go back, for I would see again
Mountains less vast, a less abundant plain,
The northern cliffs, clean-swept with driven foam,
And the rose-garden of my gracious home.

THE END.